To God; my children, Chade, CJ, Christian and Kevin; and to my wife, Mayra.

Mayra, you and our beautiful children are my everything and always will be! I smile because of you. I cry because of you. I thrive because of you. My strength comes from you.

Thank you for allowing me to take you out on that first date and eventually granting me your hand in marriage. I cherish every moment I spend with you and will love you until the last breath of air I inhale.

Going From Undisciplined to Self-Mastery
by Harris Kern
with Roger Bengtsson

© Copyright 2014 by Harris Kern

ISBN 978-1-7328303-8-7

Published by

Café con Leche

3 Griffin Hill Court
The Woodlands, TX. 77382
281-465-0119
www.cafeconlechebooks.com

GOING FROM UNDISCIPLINED TO SELF-MASTERY

FIVE SIMPLE STEPS TO GET YOU THERE

Dozens of Individual and Organizational Case Studies
The Proof, Not the Hype

HARRIS KERN

With Roger Bengtsson

Café con Leche

TABLE OF CONTENTS

FOREWORD

I was contacted by Roger Bengtsson after he searched the Internet using the keywords *self-discipline* and *mentor*. He sent me the following email:

> "I'm not proud about my self-discipline lately. Too much television, no regular sleep rhythm, and so on. I'm ashamed. Not long ago I had self-discipline and I felt fine and I probably had my best days in life. And now, back to zero again. No goals, no hunger for a new day."

He had other challenges:
❏ Severe procrastination
❏ Too much sleep—nine to ten hours
❏ Wasted two to three hours lounging around in bed every day
❏ No motivation
❏ No sense of urgency
❏ No energy

His career was going nowhere. He was a security guard in Sweden. At age forty-two his life seemed pretty dismal. His only consolation—he wasn't alone. Most people I meet have very little, if any, self-discipline. No matter how intelligent or creative someone is, without discipline, it is almost impossible to excel in life. That's why the self-help industry is a multi-billion dollar gold mine. So-called experts know that very few people become successful just by reading a book, listening to motivational audios or attending a seminar on success.

Roger was no different: he had read several self-help books and was constantly listening to audios for inspiration. Everything he tried was a short-term fix. He needed more than canned advice. He needed a mentor who walked the talk, had a time-tested process and who could hold him accountable for his daily routines. He needed a roadmap—not a lecture.

Although we lived on different continents, I felt that I could turn his life around. This book is designed to transform you similarly from an undisciplined casualty of bad habits, like Roger had been, into a master of your own fate. It will walk you through the time-proven five steps needed to become more productive and enthusiastic about life. These easy-to-follow steps will help you develop the self-discipline you'll need to live the rest of your life in a constant state of high level enthusiasm and purpose. Once you master all five of these steps, you will be able to combat the top issues affecting many people in the world today—I refer to them as The Dirty Dozen:

1. Severe procrastination
2. Failed goals
3. No motivation
4. No sense of urgency
5. Disorganization
6. Lack of structure
7. Lack of focus
8. Suboptimal sleep
9. Poor performance
10. Poor time management
11. Lack of energy
12. Inconsistency

Even though this may seem like quite a list, really it's just the tip of a very large iceberg. Individuals the world over are struggling every day to do more with less.

For your benefit, this book is divided into three major sections.
❏ Executive Overview, highlighting all five steps with simple flow diagrams and brief descriptions.

❏ The five steps, described in detail.
❏ The Proof (not the hype) helps individuals and organizations get structured with:
  • Easy-to-follow process flow diagrams of the five steps.
  • Case studies from dozens of one-on-one life coaching sessions and actual organization consulting engagements from Fortune 500 companies.
  • Multiple examples and exercises to help you get proficient in time management.
  • Exercises to help you train your mind and hold yourself accountable.

In the event you are wondering just who would buy this book, consider:
❏ Every dieter, who can't stick to a plan
❏ Everyone who wants to get into shape, but lacks the motivation
❏ Every college student going out into the world for the first time
❏ Every job seeker looking for that edge
❏ Sales managers who want to get more out of their team
❏ Real estate agents who need to remain disciplined through slow periods
❏ Companies that need to be more cost-effective
❏ Pretty much anyone or any organization that wants to be more productive

Going from Undisciplined to Self-Mastery describes how to acquire the most important ingredient for optimal success in one's lifetime: Discipline. Those who are willing to work hard to acquire discipline will not have aspirational roadblocks.

What does it look like? How does this system work? Turn the page to see how I plotted a path for Roger.

In the first half of the table below, I documented the actions taken to mentor Roger, and in the second half of the Table are the results attained from our one-on-one mentoring sessions.

Action Taken	
1	I facilitated an assessment of Roger over Skype. I asked approximately one hundred questions covering every area of his personal and professional life. The first step was to understand his strengths, weaknesses and goals. Once I completed my discovery exercise, we reviewed my findings and discussed a strategy to move forward. After the evaluation we established three priorities: career, health and relationships (family and girlfriend).
2	I designed a strategy based on his goals and three new priorities. The strategy also included mentoring him to develop his self-discipline skills using the five steps highlighted in this book: 1. Institute Structure 2. Life Prioritization 3. Time Management 4. Accountability 5. Search for Perfection
3	We established a new routine to help Roger be more productive. I wanted him to treat every day equally. My objective was to eventually train his mind so he could hold himself accountable. The routine included: • Training seven days a week. • Writing thirty minutes a day. • Practicing English daily. • Following and maintaining his to-do list every day! • Maintaining structure throughout the day. • Reducing sleep time from nine hours a day to six. • Eliminating lounging in bed. • Waking up with a purpose. • Focusing on daily milestones not his goals.
4	I continuously reminded him that it's now or never, that the old Roger was dead and gone. He needed to quickly make up for the years of laziness. I wanted to instill a sense of urgency.
5	I made sure he created a to-do list each evening.
6	I held Roger accountable several times a day, even though he resided in Sweden, using Skype calls and email. We reviewed his milestones—what worked and what didn't work.
7	I trained him to follow the same routine and to-do list and constantly reminded him that he didn't want to go back to the lazy and unproductive Roger. We had many conversations throughout the week to ensure ongoing success.
Results	
1	Roger is productive every day.
2	He trains each day.
3	He writes consistently, both blogs and books.

4	He holds himself accountable.
5	He makes every minute count: • No longer watches TV for hours at a time. • Doesn't lounge around in bed. • Doesn't procrastinate.
6	New goals are thoroughly planned with realistic milestones.
7	He's always organized and clutter-free, which allows him to be creative and even more productive.

How it Started

My neighbor, Jim Jarman, was in his forties when I was thirteen. What a specimen: intelligent, handsome, exercised every day, great physique. I looked up to him.

On one of those typical warm summer California days, Jim was outside mowing the lawn with his shorts on and his shirt off. We would always be clowning around together, trading sarcasm. On this particular day, he said the five magic words to me that changed my life forever: "Harris, you look like shit."

I could tell immediately that he was serious. He was right. I knew it. At the time, I stood six feet tall and weighed one hundred thirty-five pounds. If I turned sideways, you would not be able to see me. I was that skinny.

I looked at Jim and said that I knew it, but genuinely did not know what to do about it. I ate everything in sight but could never gain a pound. "Harris," he said, "eating massive amounts of food is not the way to approach your problem. Your body needs a major overhaul, and it doesn't start with your mouth." At thirteen, I did not understand what he was trying to tell me. How else did you gain weight?

"If you decide to follow my instructions to the letter, I will help you out."

I said "sure," not having a clue as to what was forthcoming.

"I want you here every Monday, Wednesday, and Friday after school. What time do you usually get home?"

"I get home at three-forty-five each afternoon."

"Okay, on those three days, I want you at my house by four, and don't be a minute late. If you're late, the deal is off—no second chances." This was Saturday, so we started that Monday.

I was really looking forward to my first session. Maybe, just maybe, I could obtain a body like his in no time.

What a rude awakening. He put me through hell! A very stern exercise program. What do I mean by stern? Three days a week of torture, always pushing me harder than the week before. There was weight training, running, swimming and, most importantly, lecturing. He would always keep me focused on the exercise and our long-term objective. It was continuous badgering. There was no time or place for social talk.

He would also teach me not to rely on anyone for help. Why not? Is it not okay to rely on your friends occasionally? Not for acquiring *discipline*. It is 100 percent you and no one else. Athletes know that 80 percent is in the mind, where it all starts, especially on those days that you're too tired or stressed out and not in the mood—that's when you need to push yourself the most. He was training my mind more than my body, although I did not know it at the time.

Jim was like a drill sergeant. He was instilling me with discipline. I figured if he was willing to give up his precious time to help me out, the least I could do was show up on time. Besides, after I agreed to do this, he actually dared me to quit or show up late. He tested me every day.

Looking back now, I realize what an illusory mind game this entire ordeal was. His tactic was very effective, scaring me into never being late. I did not know it back then, but he was training my mind, starting with the easiest form of discipline: punctuality.

Do you realize how difficult it was for a thirteen-year-old kid to pull this off? Think back to the number of distractions you had to deal with as a young teen. Yet I never missed a day.

Walking the Talk

There are many successful self-help gurus out there with publications. What sets me apart is that I have walked the talk for decades, and even now, in my sixties, I still seethe with passion to accomplish and excel. For me, life is all about accomplishments and leaving behind a legacy.

I am highly successful at that. My children and the love of my life, Mayra, will benefit from more than just a hefty bank account. They will inherit prime real estate and multiple businesses. They will also have a vast collection of books I authored in the family library and vivid photographs on the mantle to remember me by. I hope they will continue to abide by the morals their mother and I instilled in them. I also hope they will adhere to the same top three priorities that I did, and continue to develop their self-discipline so they'd wake up every morning for the rest of their lives *with a purpose*. Just like their dear old dad, I want them to accomplish as much as possible *every* day. Faith, balance, and discipline will always be the catalyst for their own success.

Looking back over my sixty-plus years, I remember plenty of major accomplishments. One of the things I'm most proud of is that by age sixteen, I purchased *in cash* a new car and paid for my own insurance. My disciplined mannerisms and tendencies manifested at an early age. At thirteen, I threw myself into the labor market with a vengeance. I desired money and truckloads of it—quickly, especially after having netted approximately $700 in cash, checks and bonds at my bar mitzvah in 1967.

To appease my never-ending hunger for money, I worked multiple jobs after school and on weekends. There was no job big or small that I wouldn't do: yard work, babysitting, delivering newspapers, filing brochures at a travel agency. At one time, I even worked at an auto junkyard pulling batteries from old clunkers. It was a dirty and dangerous job, but someone had to do it. I'll never forget the day that I pulled out a battery from a car right before it was hoisted up for demolition. As I stood there and watched it being lifted by a crane, a large rattlesnake fell out. I never went back after that.

These jobs were all performed between the ages of thirteen and sixteen, with 100 percent of the income being deposited into my savings account. It was the only way I could purchase a new car by my sixteenth birthday. Growing up, I was mentored to be frugal and save money. My parents always used to tell me, "Never purchase small insignificant items like records, beer, media paraphernalia, and knick-knacks at the mall. Forget all about the latest craze and always eat at home." Their sound advice has served me well.

While other teenage boys were busy scamming for girls or getting into all kinds of trouble, I had already entered the corporate world. I was only eighteen when I accepted an entry-level position in the information technology (IT) department of a large company in San Carlos, California. Back in 1972, it was referred to as Data Processing and shortly thereafter as Management Information Systems (MIS). Removing the carbon sheets from computer-generated printouts wasn't exactly a glamorous job, but it was the proverbial *foot in the door* that I needed to gain full admittance into the very exciting world of technology.

It was a full-time job, but I completed my duties in approximately five hours each day. The rest of my day was spent helping out in other departments—learning, growing and striving to get on management's radar as a quick learner, an efficient worker and someone who had a ton of initiative. My goal was to be promoted—the sooner, the better. I had bigger fish to fry.

As long as I live, I'll never forget what my dad said to me at an early age. "Son, if you rent an apartment or house it's like flushing your hard-earned money down the toilet." Needless to say, I took these words to heart. Living on my own became a goal, one that turned into reality at the age of nineteen when I purchased a home in the San Francisco Bay Area.

My life changed drastically when I bought my first home without any financial assistance. It was a two-bedroom townhome about fifteen minutes south of San Francisco. I was scared to death of getting tied down to a mortgage at such a young age. However, it was a fairly conservative strategy: putting down 20 percent so the monthly payments wouldn't strap me down. Investing in property at an early age was one of my smartest undertakings. After two years, I sold it for a nice profit and moved to a nicer neighborhood.

After dabbling in real estate, I turned my focus to muscle cars. There were millions of nice muscle cars out there, but I wanted to have so much more than just another fancy hot rod. What I yearned for was something that would win "Best of Class" at all the premier car shows in the U.S. At the age of twenty-one, I saw my muscle car and speedboat, with their matching maroon with flames paint jobs, featured on the front cover of the July 1975 issue of *Hot Rod Magazine*.

The two vehicles were showcased at the granddaddy of all car shows in Oakland, California. They won the top prize—best of show. I named the boat *Dirty Harry* and the car *Sano SS*. I received the phone call from *Hot Rod Magazine* a few weeks later. A representative had seen the car and boat at the show and wanted to feature them in one of the magazine's summer issues. Wow, what a great feeling when it hit newsstands. I'll never forget driving in my award-winning muscle car to the lakes throughout California with matching speedboat in tow to water-ski. I made quite a spectacle cruising on the streets and highways.

Early in my career, I knew that management was the right path to take. After all, that was where the big bucks were, along with once-in-a-lifetime opportunities and character-building challenges. Good communication skills, constant strategic thinking, excellent leadership skills and passion for developing a highly efficient organization was my true calling. At the age of twenty-three, I was promoted to my first management position. From that point on, I climbed the corporate ladder at a nearly record-setting pace and became vice president of IT in my early thirties.

By the time I reached my thirty-eighth birthday in 1992, I was financially set—*a multi-millionaire*. I invested wisely—mostly in property—worked hard, and never put all my eggs in one basket. I made sure there was always a steady stream of income from several small consulting firms—just in case that big *reduction in force* happened.

In 1982, my corporate job of ten years ended abruptly—everyone was given a pink slip, including yours truly. Being unemployed for the first time in my professional life was downright scary, but having a healthy savings account and multiple sources of income to pay the mortgage and living expenses for approximately two years eased the burden considerably. In a matter of a few months, I was recruited by a large Japanese electronics company in Silicon Valley.

Once I got back into the corporate world, my goal was for the name *Harris Kern* to become synonymous with IT and self-discipline. At the time, based on my research, there were many one-book wonders. But that wasn't going to cut the mustard with me. My first IT related book was published in 1994 by Prentice Hall and it quickly became a best-seller. Shortly thereafter, the president of Prentice Hall called to congratulate me and he asked me, "When are you going to write another book?" Little did he know that my mind was already actively strategizing a series of IT management how-to books.

I was invited to attend a conference in 1997, facilitated by Prentice Hall in San Diego, California. Top-level publishing executives attended, including my executive editor and his boss. My objective was to get my own imprint of books named Harris Kern's Enterprise Computing Institute. I presented my plan to them with conviction and they agreed. Over the next few weeks we hammered out a contract. The imprint published its first book in the series in 1997. It worked flawlessly, with dozens of new books being published under my imprint on a regular basis. Overall, I published more than forty books with Prentice Hall and a few other publishers as well.

I Will *Never* Stop Seeking Perfection

Why not let up? Don't I deserve it? Status quo is not living; it's merely existing. At the age of sixty I'm still sleeping four hours a night (by choice), exercising an hour and a half a day (weight lifting and cardio) and working full-time as a life coach, business consultant, author, publisher, father and husband. I will *never* let up because I love life and am passionate about helping people and organizations be productive. I now get hired by companies and individuals seeking success, or to improve on it, but lacking a path to find it. I put them on that Yellow Brick Road called *Discipline*. Why should anyone stop waking up with a purpose? Accomplish, learn and grow.

INTRODUCTION

THE DISCIPLINE ENGINE

The most important ingredient in one's life is discipline. With it, you can achieve everything; without it, you will struggle to exist. It's the motor that carries us forward; the more discipline you have, the bigger your engine. Without discipline, you stall.

Once you attain discipline, you cannot let it be shattered regardless of any obstacle or turmoil in your life. It is a tool to help you overcome the challenge and accomplish whatever you desire. It is also so much more.

Discipline brings with it a new outlook on life. Even if you have a bad day or week, discipline will keep you positive and focused on your goals—not your setbacks. The worse things get, the more discipline will motivate you. It harnesses negative attitudes into a mannerism that helps you stay focused and positive.

Discipline is a contract with yourself, a contract you must adhere to regardless of the circumstances. You are the cop: break the rules and you fail. It also inarguably alters your personality, making you more sensitive, sincere, polite, cordial and caring. Discipline is a motivational engine.

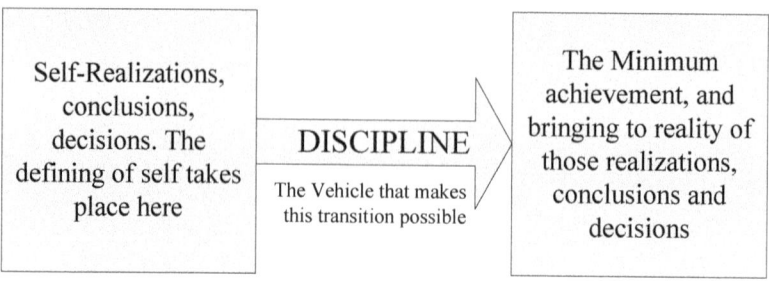

As a performance expert for life and business I am typically engaged by my clients to improve their efficiency. Each such engagement begins with a thorough evaluation of individuals (non-professionals, management and hourly staff). I assess strengths, weaknesses, goals, self-discipline (often expressed as goal and time management), leadership skills, communication practices, habits, current lifestyle, career objectives, financial management, family issues, health and relationship management. The data from the assessment becomes the foundation for designing the proper strategy and roadmap to improve performance.

Executives have very little time, little bandwidth, and almost no patience. Therefore, I created something visual they could grasp easily. I synthesized the key points of the assessment without diluting them. I call this visual queue the *Maturity Model.* Using it, you can master every part of your life.

Maturity Model

After years of coaching others on self-improvement, I realized that discipline was not static. It exists on a spectrum ranging from inadequate at the bottom to mastery at the top.

I also noticed that while a person might have discipline at work they might also be failing in their personal life. I wanted something that would show me at a glance where someone was at on this spectrum and could serve as a reminder, a kick in the ass if you will, to stay on track. So for those of you who are visual and need reminders, I created this Maturity Model. A copy is included in Appendix A, so you can print it out and put it on a mirror, a bulletin board or a computer screen to help you stay the course.

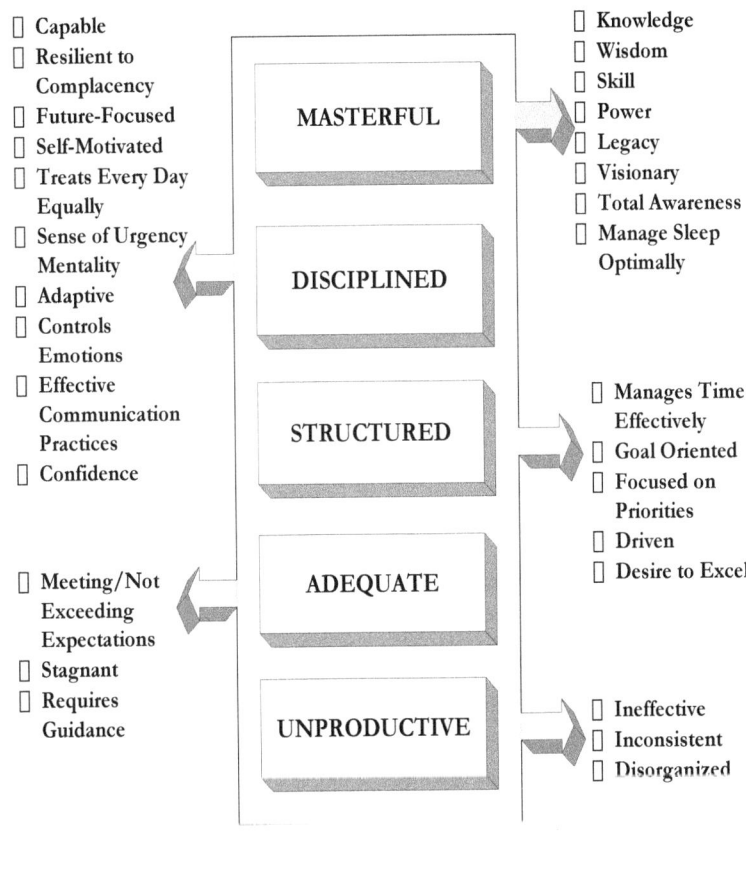

Let's take a closer look at the attributes that define each of the levels above:

Maturity Level=UNPRODUCTIVE
❑ **Ineffective:** You never accomplish goals and you're unproductive. You attempt to start new goals, but you quickly lose focus and failure is imminent, typically due to:
  • Poor time management

- Poor goal management
- Lack of sense of urgency
- Lack of motivation

❏ **Inconsistent:** Everything you do is sporadic. You start something and then quit (e.g., a new exercise routine or diet).

❏ **Disorganized:** Whether it's your home, car, garage, office, email, files—nothing is in its rightful place and it takes you twice as long to find something.

Maturity Level=ADEQUATE

❏ **Meeting/Not exceeding expectations:** You're doing the bare minimum each day—just enough to get by.

- You want to be successful, but, unfortunately, you have no desire to put forth the extra effort to achieve this.
- You procrastinate and waste an exorbitant amount of time.

❏ **Stagnant:** You aren't growing. You exist to eat, sleep and pay the bills.

❏ **Requiring guidance:** You typically need assistance to get over some of the obstacles life puts in front of you.

Maturity Level=STRUCTURED

❏ **Effective at time management:** You value your most precious resource and make every minute count.

- You're efficient with your resources (time and energy).
- You're structured:
    - Your clothes are selected the night before.
    - Your to-do list is followed religiously.
    - Your efficient routine is adhered to daily.
    - You're very organized (in terms of home, office, garage, files, desk, email, etc.).

❏ **Goal-oriented:** You're focused on your daily milestones (tasks and obligations you need to accomplish).

- You're always thinking of how to accomplish things in a more efficient manner.
- You have backup plans for each goal—just in case of an emergency.

❏ **Focused on priorities:** You live life by adhering to your priorities every day of the year. Anything that's not related to your priorities is secondary.

❏ **Driven:** You're constantly pushing yourself to accomplish more.

❏ **Wanting to excel:** You love accomplishments and always want to achieve more. You're longing to be successful at all costs. You'll do whatever it takes to achieve that objective.

Maturity Level=DISCIPLINED

❏ **Capable:** You have what it takes to do anything you desire (physically and mentally).

❏ **Not complacent:** You're never satisfied. The wheels in your mind are always turning. You can never take a prolonged break.

❏ **Future-focused:** You never think about what needs to be done today—that was already planned the night before. Your mind is always thinking ahead (e.g., tomorrow, next week and next month).

❏ **Self-motivated:** You push yourself 24-7-365.

❏ **Treating every day equally:** Your mind has been trained by treating every day equally—you:
  • Adhere to a routine.
  • Abide by your priorities.
  • Remain structured.
  • Exercise daily.
  • Manage time effectively.
  • Establish and follow a to-do list.

❏ **Having a sense of urgency:** You can act upon things (e.g., tasks, projects, milestones) in your life that help you achieve your goals at an accelerated pace.

❏ **Adaptive:** You have the creative ability to process your thoughts relating to your surroundings for beneficial reasons or to find a better solution to a difficult situation (e.g., small, big, extremely complex, highly political, cultural).

❏ **Emotionally controlled:** Whether you've had a good day or a bad day, you know how to control your emotions. You won't get too excited if you had a great day or too depressed if you had a bad one. You'll stay on an emotional even keel and redirect any negative emotions into your priorities as a positive force of energy.

❑ **Effective at communication:** You possess excellent written and verbal communication skills.

❑ **Confidence:** You believe in your ability (physically and mentally) to achieve anything you desire. You feel like you will succeed in whatever venture or goal you initiate.

  • You feel superior to most.
  • You are not negatively influenced by others.

Maturity Level=MASTERFUL

❑ **Leadership:** You possess extraordinary leadership skills. You are respected and admired. People listen to you, follow you and deliver great results for you.

❑ **Knowledge:** You possess above-average IQ, EQ and street smarts (common sense).

❑ **Wisdom:** Your wisdom is recognized. Individuals and organizations seek your advice because of your insight on many different subjects—events, people, politics. You have the ability to apply actions based on your knowledge, experience and success.

❑ **Skillful:** You possess unique skills. You can:

  • Assess difficult situations and produce solutions.
  • Resolve conflicts.
  • Think outside the box.
  • Manage difficult personalities.
  • Manage finances effectively.
  • Mentor others to be successful.

❑ **Powerful:** You feel invincible. You possess physical strength and mental toughness. You feel like a machine that never breaks down—almost robotic.

❑ **Legacy solidified:** My definition of legacy is having lived a successful life with many accomplishments, not just material possessions and money, but things that will have an impact on many people. Your spouse, family, friends and others you don't currently know will have much more than just memories to enjoy. They will all benefit from your accomplishments, wisdom and mentoring.

❑ **Visionary:** You always seek perfection in your personal and professional life by strategizing to achieve great things in less time. You constantly ask yourself "How can I achieve my goals faster?" You can see where you are going, know what's up ahead and avert obstacles along the way. You skillfully navigate the path to success.

❏ **Totally aware:** You are cognizant of everything around you. I'm not talking about physical location, but anything that could affect (negatively or positively) your priorities and goals.

❏ **Managing sleep optimally:** Your mind is trained to sleep less and to get out of bed quickly. You no longer lounge around and waste precious minutes.

The qualities in the *Structured, Disciplined* and *Masterful* levels are very powerful. If you possess them you can pretty much guarantee a successful life. With these traits you will also maintain values, be genuine, and have good relationships with business colleagues, friends, family and God.

On the next page I've included a graphic overview of those three most important levels for success. I've also noted the qualities you need to possess for each level.

What Does It Take To Master Your Life?

MASTERFUL

- You possess extraordinary leadership skills.
- You will leave behind a legacy.
- Sleep is managed optimally (fewer hours and not lounging around in bed).
- You have wisdom. Individuals and organizations will seek your advice.
- You have complete control of your life.
- You have the ability to assess difficult situations and produce solutions.
- You're well respected.
- You will always be seeking perfection.
- You will feel mentally and physically superior

DISCIPLINED

- Your mind is trained
  - You're living life with a sense of urgency.
  - Your emotions are controlled. Negative emotions are re-directed.
  - You're focused on your priorities.
  - You're consistently holding yourself accountable.
- You're treating everyday equally.
- You're always strategizing to improve.
- You're training your mind to hold yourself accountable
  - Establishing a contract.
  - Establishing key phrases.
  - Repeaingt phrases numerous times each day.

STRUCTURED

- Manage time effectively
  - Know your numbers (where time is currently utilized).
  - Establish baseline numbers for success (the most critical activities).
  - Limiting TV, video games and surfing the internet.
  - Extrapolate wasted minutes.
- Prioritize your life and learn to say no effectively.
- Remain organized (home, email, office, etc.).
- Treat everyday equally
  - Follow your 'to-do' list.
  - Follow your routine.
  - Exercise daily (some form of exercise).

UNPRODUCTIVE   ADEQUATE

Who knows how high you can climb the stairway to mastery? How badly do you want to be successful? If you apply the principles in this book you will master your life. I have written four additional books to help you make that journey:

DISCIPLINE: *Six Steps to Unleashing Your Hidden Potential.* In this book, I describe the six steps to acquiring discipline and what it can do for you. I also highlight the difficulties in acquiring discipline and what it takes to overcome those obstacles.

DISCIPLINE: *Training the Mind to Manage Your Life.* I depict how individuals can train their minds. Understanding how to train the mind is one of the most important aspects of acquiring discipline. Once your mind is trained, it will hold you accountable to your daily obligations, goals, critical milestones and it WILL ensure you abide by your priorities.

DISCIPLINE: *Mentoring Children for Success.* My co-authors and I educate you on how to mentor your own kids to be successful. Children must acquire discipline to manage their myriad activities, set and achieve goals, and be successful in their lives. But few kids today are being equipped with the necessary tools to make discipline a cornerstone of their daily routine. And few adults know specifically how to help them. The third in the series, this book articulates both the *why* and the *how* of discipline for children.

DISCIPLINE: *Take Control of Your Life.* Companies are cutting back all over the world. This means that you, the employee, will be doing the work of two or more people, or you might be looking for work. How will you manage your workload? How will you maintain your sanity? How will you keep your health? How will you find time for your family? You're in a fifteen-round fight every day just to survive. Discipline is the tool you use to pick yourself back up and live to fight another day. This book simplifies the complex process of discipline into ten easy to remember methods and evaluation criteria that, *if applied,* will improve your life. Truly, it is a Ten Commandments of discipline.

My goal with all of my books is to educate people on the power of self-discipline to help individuals excel in every facet of life. Unfortunately, learning about it and acquiring it are two different ball games. Anyone can learn it, but to instill it into your daily routine takes a lot of effort and sacrifice. Acquiring discipline is not a one-week course someone can take over the Internet and receive a diploma. It's hard work and there are obstacles, but the benefits by far outweigh the sacrifices.

Acquiring discipline begins with organizing every aspect of your life. The more organized you are, the less clutter you have; therefore, you remain focused on your goals and are not distracted by clutter.

The Long and Winding Road to Discipline

When I first tried to publish this book, I was told that my steps were too painstaking for the average person. "Most people will not be able to stick with your approach. They will be turned off and not buy your book." I don't disagree. Discipline is *very* hard work. Very few will achieve the highest levels of personal development in their lifetime, but many can excel and certainly improve their lives.

Answer this question: *Why do so many people who attempt to seek a more productive life fail?* They've read many self-help books, listened to inspirational audios, attended seminars on success, yet they still can't achieve their goals. Wake up, world! The so-called and often-marketed *simple techniques* are not the answer. If it was a simple process everyone would be disciplined. No one needs to be Einstein to dispute that logic.

The Disclaimer

Every client I've mentored would receive a disclaimer before we began work. I would explain to them: "*Acquiring discipline is not a one-month endeavor. It could take three to six, perhaps a year or longer. No two people are alike. Also, being disciplined is not a nine-to-five, Monday-Friday, one-hour a week lecture session. To acquire discipline, there are no boundaries or time limitations. If you have poor time management in your personal life, chances are you have poor time management in your professional world. It's up to you—how badly do you want success? If you want it, then understand that there will be many sacrifices along the way. Your lackadaisical lifestyle will certainly be impacted. Initially (typically the first thirty days) it's going to be a tough transition. You will need to push beyond your limitations like never before. You've rarely pressed yourself in the past, but now, because you want to accomplish your goals, your old lifestyle needs to change once and for all. Is this doable? Yes I will be attached to your hip and we WILL be successful."* The super-achiever will have an easier time adapting to this rigor than the underachiever.

If my sole purpose is to sell books, then I will fail miserably. If I wanted to sell millions of copies I would *really* sugar-coat my approach and *minimize* the effort. That's the objective of most self-help books. This is why the self-help industry is thriving with promise and hope. If you want the key ingredient for success, then unfortunately, you will need to earn it; there's *no* simplified version. There is, however, a formula for success. Following my five steps is that formula.

Managing the Force

Being disciplined means effectively managing every aspect of your life. You've made it to the big leagues. You're in *complete* control of your life. Right? Well sort of. Initially, your disciplined mannerisms control you.

When you first become disciplined, you will know it. You become robot-like. Your routine becomes habitual. You are *extremely* focused, almost too focused on your daily milestones. You live life with urgency every minute of the day. Nothing can break your resolution! You're now that drill sergeant holding yourself accountable—every hour of every day. There's no letting up. All you care about are accomplishments. The more the better. You have all the power. Initially, this is a good thing, because before you started this journey you were unproductive and a failure in many areas of your life. Much of your time on this planet was squandered. You needed to turn your life around quickly.

Here's the big question: *Do we all need to be like drill sergeants all the time?* What if we don't *always* want to be disciplined? What if we just want a little bit of discipline or to only be disciplined in a certain aspect of life? Does it have to be an all or-nothing proposition?

All or Nothing

Unfortunately, or fortunately depending on how you look at it, you must acquire the full force of discipline at first. I'm not saying you need to be at the Masterful Level of the Maturity Model (See Appendix A). You do, however, need to fully develop your self-discipline skills and reach the *Disciplined* plateau of the Maturity Model. You have to acquire that power first, embrace it and then manage it to fit the lifestyle you desire. Unfortunately there is no other way, not at first. Initially, it's *all* or *nothing*.

Chill—It's Okay

Now that you're disciplined, can you ever turn it off and relax? *Yes you can.* The nice part is once you're disciplined—your self-discipline skills are fully developed. No one can take away those skills and you won't forget how to use them. You're structured for the rest of your life, you will always manage time effectively, you consistently hold yourself accountable and you will focus on your daily milestones.

If you want to sleep in a few extra hours on the weekend—go for it. If you want to take the day off and do nothing—go for it. *Now you're in control.* You can turn it off and on at will. There's no greater gift than being fully disciplined to manage your life to fit your needs.

PART I: EXECUTIVE OVERVIEW

Success is not measured by accolades, trophies or your position in society. Success is measured by your feeling of self-worth and knowing that you are putting forth your best effort each day to attain your goals. Sure, the accolades and awards are nice, but they are symbols of achievement—not of success. True success is internal. It starts and ends with yourself.

Finding success is not easy. Look at top international CEOs, famous athletes or any individual that you personally admire. Those individuals had to put in endless hours of work and show immense dedication to climb the corporate ladder, reach the highest level, or simply gain your utmost respect. Individuals may have been instrumental in your path to success, but that only takes you so far along the way. The key is internal buy-in. It starts with your *self* because you need to believe in the person you want to be and must have the desire to start. It ends with your *self* because only you know how great you can be, and only you can push yourself to reach that height. You are ultimately responsible for your own successes and failures.

If you accept that you can attain greatness, the measure of your potential success expands. The finite constant in the formula for success is time, a commodity that you cannot get back and one that you cannot artificially manufacture. Due to time's finite nature, to put your best effort forward each day, you need to make the most of each second. The constant juggling of activities and trying to do too much with too little creates obstructions and detours. *Structure* is the key to bursting through that roadblock. Structure allows you to simplify and prioritize your life. It allows you to make the most out of time; it allows you to focus your activities and direct your energy.

The first three sections of this book—*Institute Structure, Prioritize Your Life,* and *Master Time*—provide a solid foundation and a roadmap needed to accomplish your goals. Beyond that, the last two sections (*Hold Yourself Accountable* and *Seek Perfection*) provide you with the mental toughness to maintain your course and constantly push yourself to reach the pinnacle of your personal success story.

Below is a process flow of the five steps:

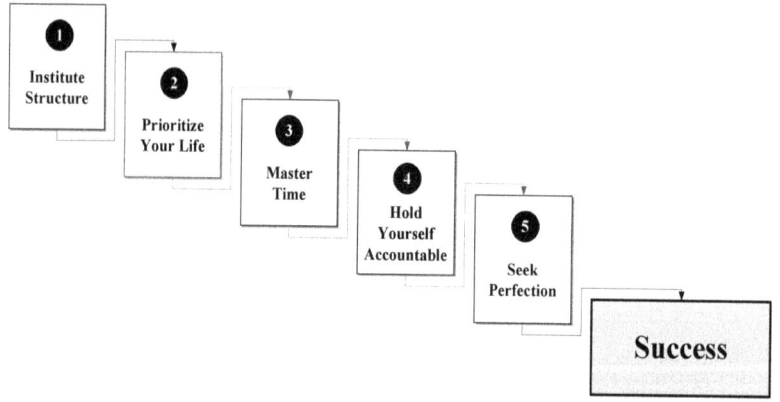

Why these steps? Why start with structure?

Without *structure* (being organized, following a routine, and your to-do list) your life would be too chaotic, therefore unproductive. If you live and work in and around unorganized environments you cannot be efficient. That also goes for your mind: when it's cluttered, you cannot effectively focus on your goals. Doesn't the path to success start by defining your goals?

Anyone can establish goals—most of you have. But how many have you accomplished? You need to first *structure* your life before you can accomplish goals consistently. Don't bother establishing goals before you *prioritize* your life. Without adhering to *priorities* you get overwhelmed, easily lose focus and eventually fail.

Most people take *time* for granted. In this section I highlight the steps to help you *master time*. I also believe that people should *manage sleep optimally*. Holding yourself *accountable* is where the rubber meets the road. Being your own cop is very difficult. However, if you learn to hold yourself *accountable* you will not fail. Your mind becomes that cop that keeps you on track. You will automatically:

❏ Be motivated
❏ Possess effective time management skills
❏ Adhere to your priorities
❏ Be organized
❏ Focus on your goals and complete them as promised

Last but not least, if you get this far, why not try to master your life by *seeking perfection?* Here's how to continue to grow in life and how to proactively monitor your activities to maintain that balance, happiness and quality of life we all desire. Let's take a closer look at the five steps:

STEP 1: INSTITUTE STRUCTURE

Below is a process flow on how to institute structure into your life.

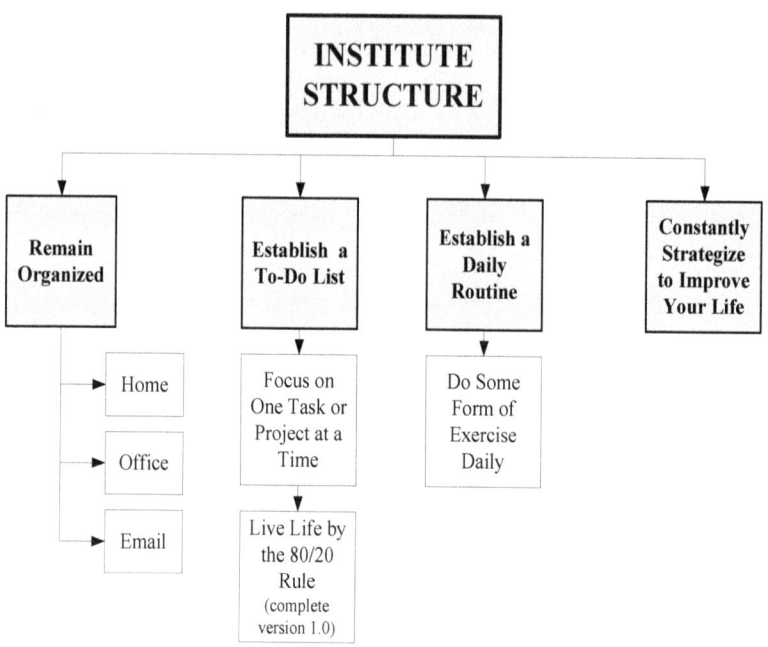

Remain Organized

Your work and home environment need to be clutter-free. That includes but is not limited to your desk, email, home and car. The more clutter you have in your view and in your mind the less productive you will be. The more organized you are, the less time you waste. The less time you waste, the more productive you are.

Establish a To-Do List Nightly

Document a list of all activities (e.g., tasks, errands, projects) the night before. You should establish one to-do list daily, which encompasses your professional and personal life. Below are some helpful tips when establishing your to-do list.

Do Not Waste Cycles in the Morning. In the morning you need to hit the ground running and execute. You need to be following your to-do list throughout the day, from the time you get up. Create a regimen and follow it precisely.

Work on Your More Brain-Intensive Activities in the Morning. You are usually more creative, resourceful and energetic in the morning. In the afternoon, people are typically more tired. Plan on doing administrative activities late afternoon and early evening. (If you are truly an afternoon or night person, adjust accordingly.)

Focus on One Task or Project at a Time. Our brain can only process one thing at a time effectively.

Live Life by the 80/20 Rule. Take your project as far as you can go. You can always go back later and take it to the next level. You don't have to complete a task to make the effort worthwhile. Eighty percent done is better than another missed or failed project. Once your project is complete, you can always revisit it to make improvements and finish.

Establish a Daily Routine

A routine is a prescribed, detailed course of action to be followed regularly, a standard procedure from the time you get up until the time you go to sleep. Document the appropriate routine. Keep it simple. The more complex it is, the more difficult it will be to follow.

Exercise Daily

Clean your apartment, walk around the block, go to the gym, wash the car, or do some other sort of activity every day. The key to being successful with your exercise routine is *change* and *consistency.* If you do something every day it becomes habitual. Doing something different keeps things a bit more exciting. Change your exercise routine frequently for better results.

Constantly Strategize

Whenever possible, think of ways to be more efficient. *How can I improve my routine? How can I complete my goals ahead of schedule? What can I do to make my business grow more effectively?*

STEP 2: PRIORITIZE YOUR LIFE

Below is a process flow on how to prioritize your life.

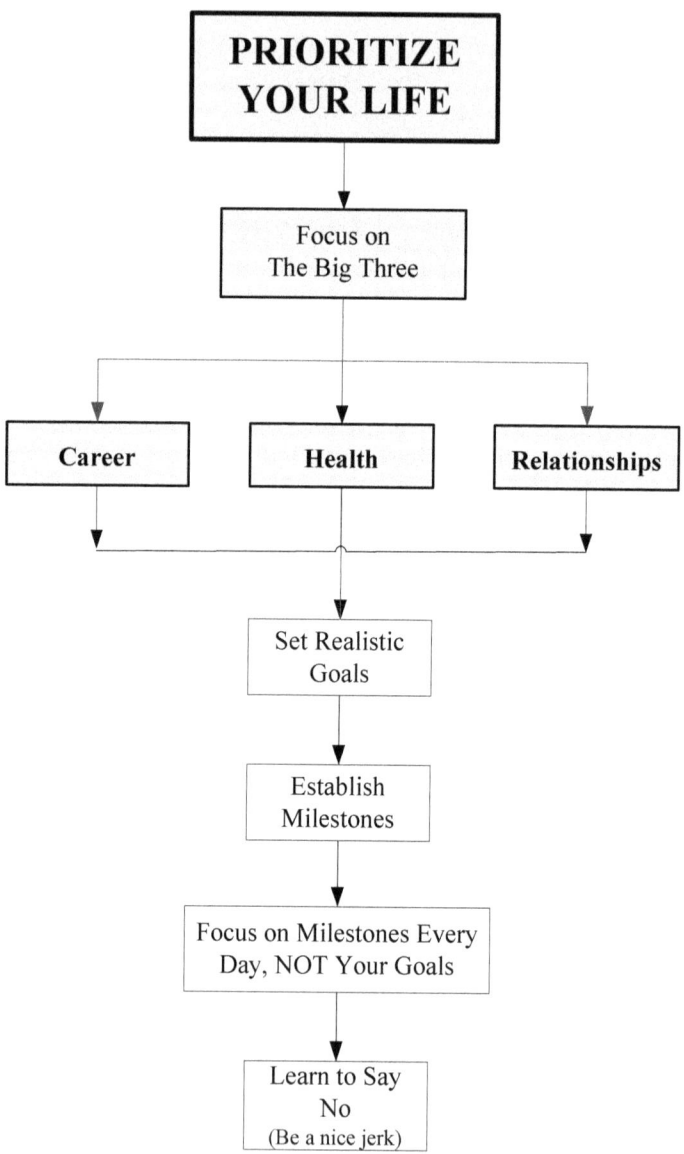

Focus on the Big Three

The three most critical priorities for success are:

- ❏ *Career:* Job, business, finances, education.
- ❏ *Health:* Exercise, weight management, lifestyle (drinking, smoking).
- ❏ *Relationships:* Managing emotions, managing your significant other, spending quality time with family, spending quality time with God, allocating time for friends and managing professional relationships.

Set Realistic Goals

Set goals that are aligned with your priorities and have realistic due dates. Be conservative in the beginning. If you take on too much, you will fail. Once you start developing your self-discipline skills, you can gradually take on more.

Establish and Focus on Milestones

Milestones are those small steps you take that will help you achieve your goals. For example, if your goal is to lose fifty pounds, what do you need to do every day to help you achieve that goal? If you focus on accomplishing your daily milestones, the goals will take care of themselves.

Learn to Say No

If you try to help everyone and take on too much, you will surely fail. People can utilize a huge chunk of your resources. Be a nice jerk.

STEP 3: MASTER TIME
Below is a process flow on how to manage time efficiently.

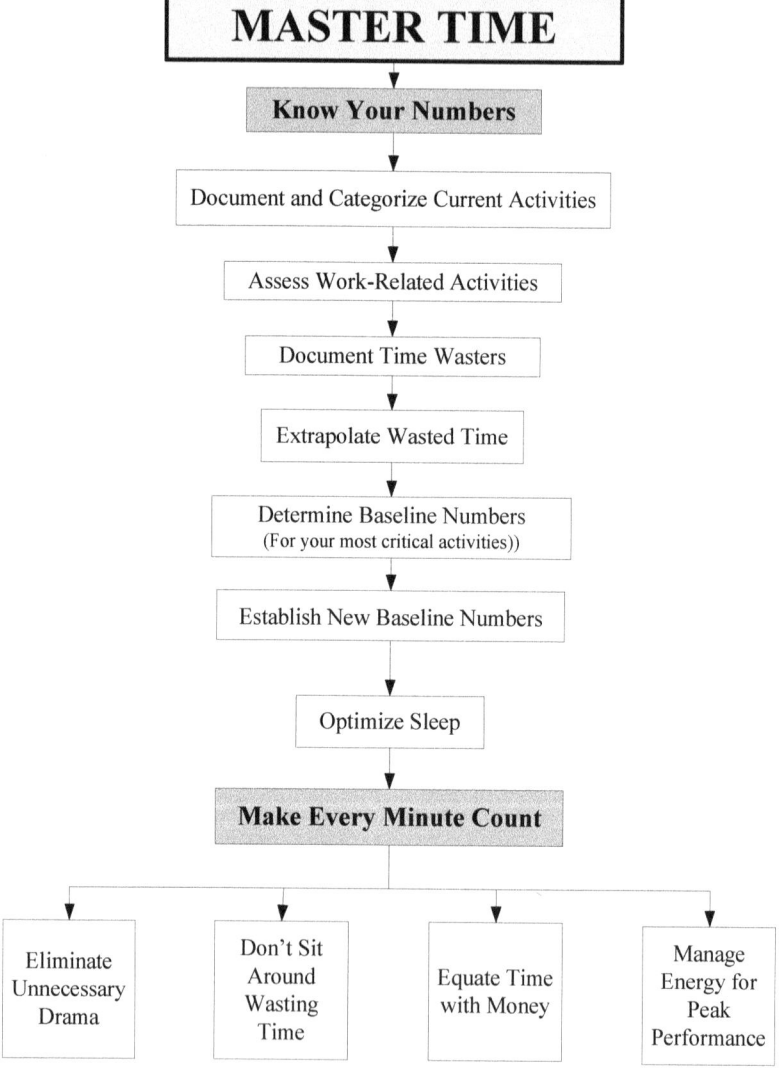

Know Your Numbers

You can't manage your life effectively unless you know your numbers. You need to know how much time you spend on each activity. Where is your time being consumed? What are your most critical activities for success? How much time should you be spending on your most critical activities?

Document and Categorize Activities

Document the start and end times of your activities in a twenty-four hour period for one week. Categorize most of your activities. You don't want to waste precious cycles being too detail-oriented. An example of a category could be *morning prep*. Don't document every little detail (e.g., brushed your teeth, went to the bathroom and shaved). Categorizing activities will help you see where the bulk of your time is spent.

Assess Work-Related Activities

Evaluate your work-related activities in detail. Work consumes more than a third of most individuals' lives. The demands are daunting. The competition is fierce. You need to produce *more* in less time. The more efficient you are, the greater the potential for a successful career.

Document Time Wasters

Sometimes we don't even know how much time we actually waste. Take the time to document where you waste most of your time. It's truly eye-opening.

Extrapolate Wasted Time

It's not about how many hours you waste on any given day, it's how many weeks or months you flush down the toilet every year. Extrapolate the minutes you waste daily throughout the year. It will shock you.

Determine Baseline Numbers

Which activities will help you be successful? Which ones are the most important to achieve daily? How much time (baseline numbers) are you currently spending on your most critical activities?

Establish New Baseline Numbers

How much time should you be spending on your most critical activities to be successful? Document those new baseline numbers.

Optimize Sleep

People waste an exorbitant amount of time because they take sleep for granted. In general, people sleep too much and mindlessly lounge in bed.

Make Every Minute Count

Learn to utilize your time efficiently. It's all about the minutes. We waste hundreds of precious minutes throughout the day. Before you go to bed, look back at the time you wasted. Some of you will have lost a good four hours of your life—some much more than that.

Eliminate Unnecessary Drama

We all know people who could be considered toxic. These toxic people can absorb enormous amounts of your time and drain your life energy. They make the same mistakes over and over again. Eliminate this distraction.

Don't Sit Around Wasting Time

Can you really afford to sit around and do nothing? I don't think so. Always be prepared to make the most of down-time like waiting for a doctor's appointment.

Equate Time with Money

Put a price on your time. You need to start realizing that your time is very valuable. How much is your time worth?

Manage Energy for Peak Performance

Execute brain-intensive activities in the morning versus late in the afternoon when you're tired. You are much more resourceful and creative in the morning and therefore more efficient.

STEP 4: HOLD YOURSELF ACCOUNTABLE

The accountability step is divided into three parts because it's important to first understand *what accountability is*, then *how to attain it*, and finally *what the end result looks like*. Let's first look at what accountability is.

What Is Accountability?

Below is a process flow on what accountability is.

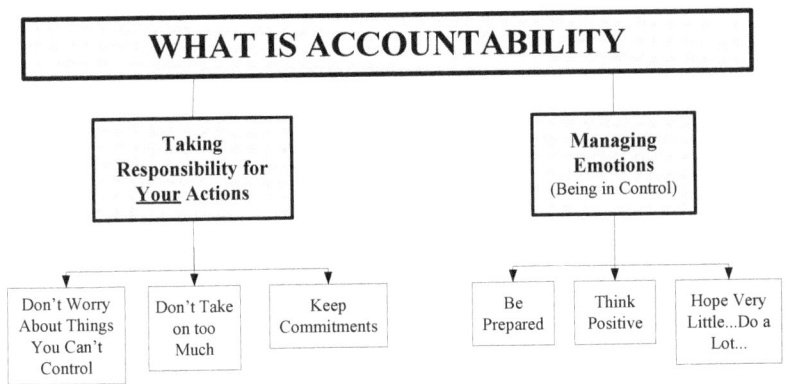

Taking Responsibility for Your Actions

Accountability means taking responsibility for your actions and keeping your commitments. Where would society be without accountability? Our society is highly efficient and depends on people to be accountable for their actions: businesses, transportation systems and schools. Without accountability there would be chaos. We have to eat and pay our bills; we have no choice. Unfortunately, accountability stops there for many.

Don't Worry About Things You Can't Control

Why bother? You waste precious cycles when there's nothing you can do about the situation? Whether it's your boss, whom you think is a dictator (and are always complaining about) or a car accident (that's not your fault), there is absolutely nothing you can do about it. You can't quit your job until you find another, and you can't stop driving. Worrying about these negative situations only wastes valuable energy and time.

Don't Take on Too Much

Be prudent about how much you take on. Don't be a *yes-person*—be a *nice jerk* instead. Be selective about how many commitments you make. You probably already have a full plate. Make sure you take on your obligations aligned with your priorities. If you have ample time at the end of the day and you're not that tired, then perhaps you can take on a few more ancillary tasks.

Keep Commitments

Commitment is the key to success with all endeavors. It cannot be halfhearted, for that is not commitment. It needs to be all out, do-or-die. Your mind and body have to want it and be completely behind it. Once you commit to something, you have to follow through, and that includes your own goals.

Managing Emotions

Negative emotions (e.g., having a bad fight with your significant other) will bring your productivity levels down and keep them down for hours, or even days. Controlling and redirecting negative emotions into a powerful positive force is crucial for success. Maintain an even-keel demeanor: do not get too excited or too upset.

❏ Be prepared for the unexpected, especially for the worst of times.

❏ Stay focused on the positive. See below for more details.

Be Prepared

Controlling your emotions means being prepared and planning for the worst case. Emergencies happen when you least expect them. The more practice you get controlling your emotions the easier it will be to cope with the unexpected.

Think Positive

There's an old saying: stay positive and good things will happen. Nice concept, but it's not always true. Sure, you *should* think positive every day of the year, but that's not realistic over the long haul. Good things *and* bad things will happen regardless of your disposition on any given day. Learn how to efficiently cope with the bad.

Hope a Little but Do a Lot

If you want a better life, successful career or strong body, stop hoping that a miracle will happen one day and start doing something about it. Hoping should not be your primary focus. The more time you spend hoping the less effort is put into strategizing and executing to improve your life.

How to Attain Accountability

Below is a process flow on how to attain accountability.

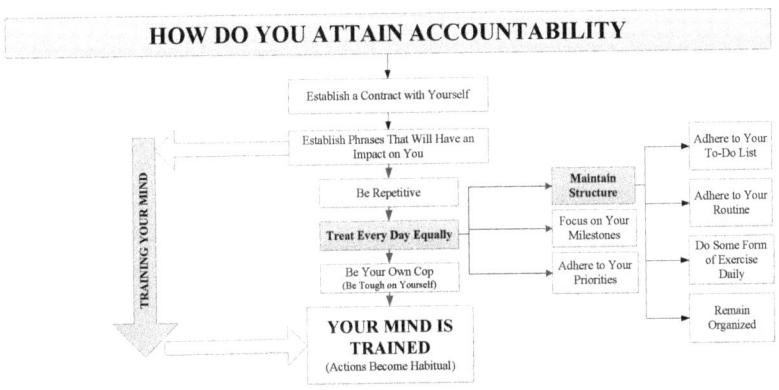

Establish a Contract with Yourself

Adhere to my five steps and establish some guidelines. How badly do you want success? Abide by your contract at all costs.

Train Your Mind

Training your mind is the single most important ingredient to consistently hold yourself accountable.

Establish Phrases

Establish phrases that will have a positive impact on your life, words easily remembered.

Be Repetitive

Repeat those phrases dozens of times each day until they become habitual. Rehearse it like you mean it—as if you were an Academy Award-winning actor.

Treat Every Day Equally

1. Adhere to your priorities and focus on your milestones first every day.
2. Adhere to your routine.
3. Do some form of exercise daily.
4. Follow your to-do list.
5. Remain organized.

Be Your Own Cop

You're the enforcer. It's difficult to be your own cop, but ask yourself this: *How badly do I want to be successful?* Practice being that tough cop until your mind is trained and it takes over those duties.

Be Tough on Yourself

If you break your rules, be unforgiving. Don't tell yourself, *It's okay, tomorrow is another day.* Be that highway patrolman that was a drill sergeant in his previous line of work.

When Your Mind Is Trained...

It becomes the enforcer. It will *always* hold you accountable even if you feel lazy or tired. Go take on the world—you have the power!

The End Result

Below is a process flow depicting the end result—when you hold yourself accountable.

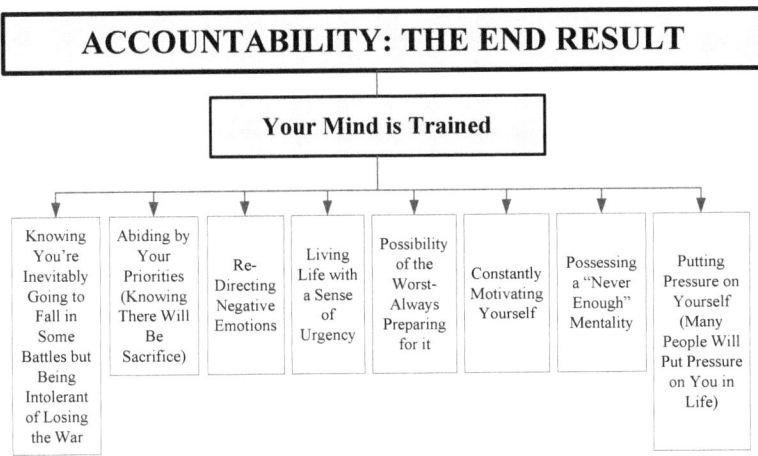

Knowing You Will Sometimes Fail

Life is a never-ending war. You're in constant battles. It's you against many obstacles—some bigger than others. Life is all about planning ahead for the inevitable and conquering those obstacles when they appear so you can eventually master every aspect of your life.

Abiding by Your Priorities

There will be plenty of distractions to derail your progress. You will only focus on obligations, tasks and projects that are associated with your priorities.

Preparing for the Worst

You will always be aware that bad things will happen. You will be ready for negative situations.

Redirecting Negative Emotions

There will be plenty of self-negativity in your lifetime. You will redirect that negativity into a positive force to help you stay focused and conquer your goals.

Living with a Sense of Urgency

Time flies. The next thing you know you're fifty years old. You look back and ask yourself: "What have I accomplished?" When your mind is trained you will no longer procrastinate. You will be extremely focused on your priorities, goals and milestones and nothing else. You will want to accomplish everything before its actual due date.

Constantly Motivating Yourself

You will stay motivated and you won't need to pick up another self-help book or attend a seminar on success.

Possessing a "Never Enough" Mentality

The more you accomplish, the more you want! You will never be satisfied!

Putting Pressure on Yourself

Life is full of stress and pressure. If you're prepared in advance for the unexpected and unrealistic (e.g., a project with an aggressive due date) you will succeed regardless of the challenge.

STEP 5: SEEK PERFECTION

Below is a process flow on how to always seek perfection.

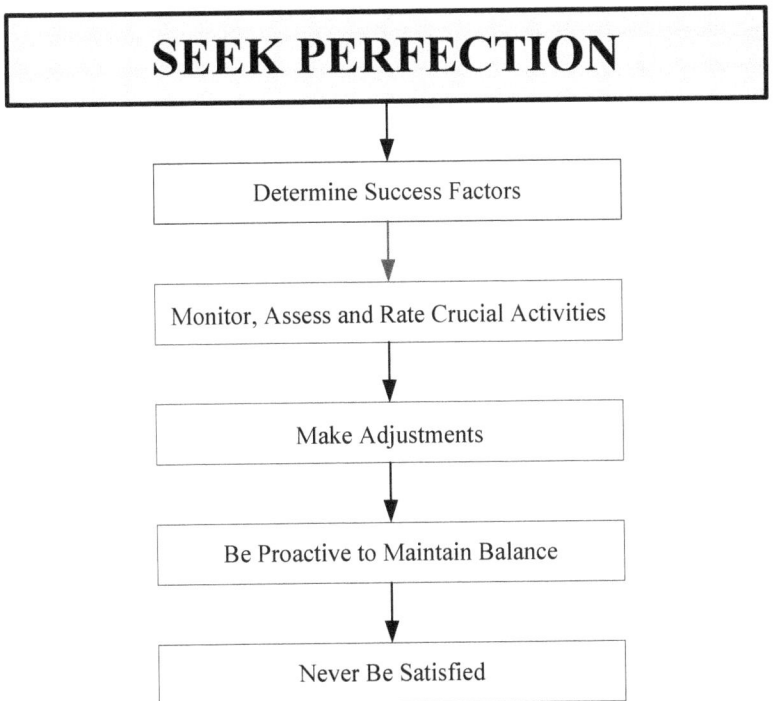

Determine Success Factors

Which activities will help you achieve success faster? Maintaining good health could be one of your most important success factors. Another could be your relationship with your significant other.

Determine Criteria for Success

If maintaining good health is a key success factor, what criteria can you monitor, assess and rate on a daily basis that would promote a healthy lifestyle? Perhaps it's what you eat that day and the quality of your exercise routine. Determine the best criteria for success for you.

Rate Each Criterion

Using a scale of 1 to 5, rate the criteria for each of your important activities. Then add them up and divide by the number of criteria to determine your score for each activity.

Adjust

For activities that are rated a 3 or below, make the appropriate adjustments. For example, if you're always starving during your workout and it's affecting the quality of this activity, eat something light before exercising.

Maintain Balance

Be proactive—gauge progress daily. This will allow you to maintain that balanced lifestyle you desire. It's easy to put too much emphasis on one activity; however, by being proactive and monitoring yourself daily you will be able to allocate your resources appropriately for all of your most important activities.

Never Be Satisfied

Never be satisfied with the level of happiness you've attained. There are always areas in our lives that need attention to keep the balance consistent. Being happy in all aspects of your life is the mother of all accomplishments. Don't settle. If you must, remember to always settle for more.

PART II: THE FIVE STEPS

STEP 1: INSTITUTE STRUCTURE

You may say, "It's bad enough that I need to have a structured routine at work, from the time I get in the car, subway or bus until the time I get home. Why would I want structure twenty-four hours a day? Wouldn't a managed lifestyle leave me more stressed out than I already am?" Now let me ask you a question. If free time is precious, wouldn't you want to have more of it to relax, to play with your kids or even more time to do nothing?

With a structured lifestyle you will gain back some of those precious minutes you currently throw away every day because you're disorganized. Those minutes will add up to hours by week's end, days by the end of the month and several weeks by the end of the year.

Don't continue to do things in a spontaneous manner. The demands on your career and personal life are huge. The more effective you are in instilling structure in every aspect of your life, the more you will accomplish in a shorter amount of time.

By instituting structure you're setting the stage to be disciplined. This is where you develop policy, change your operating basis and implement those policies and guidelines into your everyday activities. However, this is where most people stall and end up failing as they try to get their life in order. My goal is to help you develop the skills necessary to overcome the challenges of becoming structured.

Don't Set Goals… Yet

You may have reacted with surprise, skepticism and curiosity after reading this title. You've probably heard on many occasions from many people, including self-help experts, that you should always set goals first. Although just about everyone sets goals, the sad fact is that most people fail to accomplish them. Creating goals is easy. The hard part is thoroughly planning, establishing daily milestones, being persistent, executing them and then holding yourself accountable.

So what's the problem? First, many people think they're setting goals when they're really just dreaming. Dreaming involves aspiration; pursing goals requires perspiration. The reason most people don't accomplish their goals is that they're unstructured—disorganized, don't follow a routine or adhere to a to-do list. Your goals need a solid foundation and you get that when you institute structure into every aspect of your life. You can't possibly be effective if you have a mess around you and if your thoughts are distracted with clutter. You need to be organized before setting goals. Without structure you're setting yourself up for failure. Below is a process flow of how to institute structure into your life.

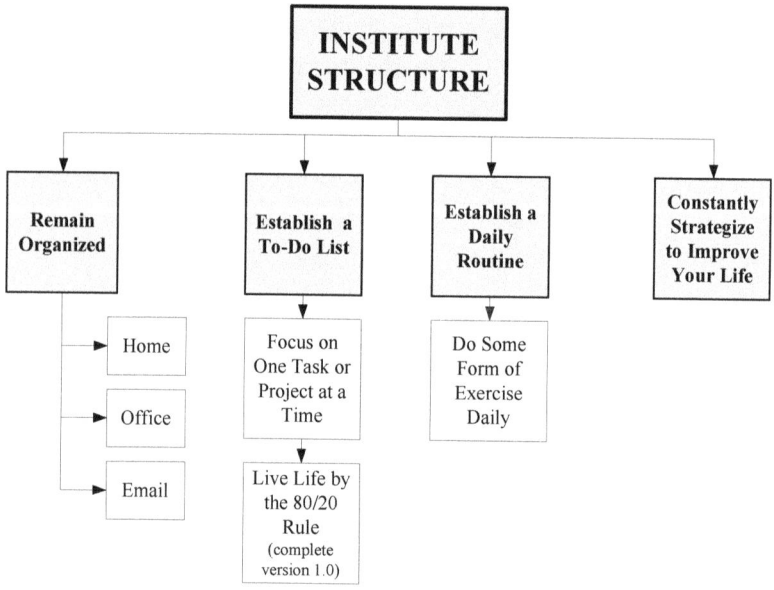

Remain Organized

The more organized you are the more efficient you become, therefore accomplishing more each day. Organizing your environment keeps your brain from overloading and shutting down. It allows you to focus on your work, not your clutter. It promotes strategic thinking and the discovery of better methods to accomplish goals. Also, when we look at a mess it has a tendency to put us in a depressed mood. When things are put away in an orderly manner, it makes us feel great.

We all know the benefits of being organized—so why don't we

just do it? The question is really quite simple to answer. People with clutter everywhere can become overwhelmed and react by pushing off tasks for another day. That day never comes. Disorganization leads to procrastination. Procrastination compounds stress. Consider the benefits of being in control of your time and space. You know where everything is. You can locate anything without putting in much physical or mental effort. You will focus ONLY on the important things, not the clutter. Being organized can save you time and money and save you from embarrassing situations, especially forgetting important dates.

Unclutter

The more clutter you're surrounded by, the more time you waste! Successful people organize every aspect of their life:

❏ Home/office

Closet

- Hang things neatly. Put everything back in the same place after using.
- Separate suits, jeans, shirts, etc.
- Prepare your work clothes the night before—it takes too long to think about what to wear in the morning.

Desk/work area

- Keep office supplies in one drawer.
- Keep the phone on your left-hand side if you are right-handed.
- Take five to ten minutes at the end of the day to keep your desk organized.
  - ✔ Update your to-do list for the next day.
  - ✔ If you are working on a high-priority project, place it in the middle of your desk.

❏ Paper management

Don't let papers pile up in stacks. Each time you handle paper ask yourself: Is it a bill or an important document? Does it have to be paid or answered in the next few weeks or does it have to be filed? Set up a step file sorter on your desk, to put documents in the following six categories, starting with the top shelf and working down.

- **Must do**—important—typically bills or important papers that need a response within days or weeks.

- **Thinking about it.**
- **Awaiting reply.**
- **Read and refer** until later.
- **Hold** indefinitely (typically until the end of the year).
- **File**—long-term (e.g., copies of tax documents, medical records, legal documents). Organize files in cabinets, storage bins or drawers as time permits.

❏ Meetings

Make sure your meetings are structured.

- Have an agenda and start the meeting promptly as advertised.
- If you have to attend someone else's meeting and your input is not required, look attentive but strategize your own projects or goals. Always carry a notepad.

❏ Whiteboard

- Maintain cleanliness and keep material current.

❏ Email

- Don't leave email sitting in your inbox. Keep it clean so it becomes an extension of your daily task list: delete unwanted emails immediately.
- Everything you need to keep should be dragged to the appropriate folder. Only emails that require immediate action should be left in your inbox for more than a day.
- Don't constantly look at your email. It can be a huge distraction. People get addicted to checking their email frequently. This isn't good, especially when you need to concentrate on a project. Schedule times to look at your email.

The Discipline of the Evening

If you struggle with getting up in the morning and attacking the day in pursuit of your goals, ask yourself whether you have demonstrated sufficient discipline in your preparation. Being well-rested and prepared is one of the central ingredients to a high level of productivity.

Your success with the day ahead is often determined by the progress and the discipline of preparation on the day prior. This is because if you wait until the morning, you are much more likely to be affected by time pressure and distractions that inevitably arise over the course of the day. By knowing what you have to do ahead of time and preparing all of the necessary tools and components to be used in executing those tasks, you overcome the hurdle of preparation early, leaving your energy and mind free to tackle the steps that count.

For instance, every builder knows that selecting the right materials and getting them to the job site is the most difficult part of any construction project. Once everything is in place, the actual execution of building the structure is fun and rewarding. If the materials are scattered, misplaced, or missing, a simple job can become a nightmare for even the most experienced professional.

Most people believe that being successful means getting up before sunrise and pushing through adversity and unpleasantness to accomplish a goal. Successful people know that while perseverance is important, clarity of purpose and simplicity are the key components of discipline that make it possible to get it done. Try the following simple steps to create the optimum conditions that will allow you to work at your best.

1. Set the evening alarm for whatever time is appropriate, leaving yourself sufficient time to go through your preparation routine.

2. At that time, clean up the workspace. A clean and organized workspace is the most critical shield against disruptive thoughts, tasks, and interruptions.

3. Prepare all the components that are to be used the next day:
   • Lay out the clothes you will wear.
   • Prepare your lunch.
   • Ready whatever tools you use the next day—computers, phones, tools, equipment, literature, research materials.

4. Reflect on the progress of the day and draw the appropriate conclusions about what was done right or what could have been done differently. This is best done on paper in a designated place. By keeping track of your day's progress, you learn to keep yourself accountable. It forces you to keep yourself focused on objective results, rather than on the amount of time you spend doing any particular thing. Lastly, it creates a written record that can be referenced for motivation. An added bonus is that it creates a nice way to track the development of your goals and progress.

5. Create a compelling vision for tomorrow. Polarize the day's progress with the bigger perspective of what you're trying to accomplish. Spend ten to twenty minutes getting clear on exactly how the things you are doing are moving you in the right direction. Try to generate excitement within yourself about the prospect of doing the things you've outlined for tomorrow.

Establish a Daily Routine

What is a routine? *A habitual way of doing things, a series of steps that you take in order to accomplish a task or goal.* What exactly do you do in a twenty-four-hour period? This is by no means a brief description but a very detailed outline of what you do with *every* minute in a day.

It begins from the moment the alarm goes off in the morning. It includes the times you spend hitting the snooze button and total elapsed time until you wake up and are vertical. Every minute needs to be documented: your commute to work, how long you spend on morning preparation—shower, dress, brush teeth, how long you watch TV on the weekdays and weekends.

You need to be on top of your days rather than your days being on top of you. If you do what you've always done, you'll settle for mediocrity and struggle to get ahead. Is it enough or can you do better? Tell yourself that you need to stop whining that you never have enough time to complete everything. I'm sure you hear the same complaints from your friends, colleagues, and family.

You could have one routine for the weekdays and another one for weekends. Routines should be flexible and not overbearing. You want consistency, not more stress in your life. A typical weekend routine could be much different, with more leisure time, but still focus on your priorities.

Below is a sample routine.

Time	Sat 1-Oct	Sun 2-Oct	Mon 3-Oct	Tue 4-Oct	Wed 5-Oct	Thu 6-Oct	Fri 7-Oct
4:30 AM			Wake up & do morning prep				
4:45 AM			Drive to the gym				
5:00 AM			Exercise				
5:15 AM							
5:30 AM							
5:45 AM			Drive back home				
6:00 AM			Shower and dress				
6:15 AM							
6:30 AM			Dress kids & make breakfast				
6:45 AM							
7:00 AM	Wake up, coffee & snack	Wake up, coffee & snack	Check email from home				
7:15 AM			Feed kids and prep for school				
7:30 AM	Take a walk around the block	Drive to the gym					
7:45 AM		Work out					
8:00 AM	Make breakfast for family						
8:15 AM	Family time						
8:30 AM			Drive to work				
8:45 AM							
9:00 AM		Make breakfast for family	Work				
9:15 AM							

9:30 AM	Do work-related email						
9:45 AM							
10:00 AM		Church & family time					
10:15 AM	Clean house						
10:30 AM							
10:45 AM							
11:00 AM	Groceries, cleaners						
11:15 AM							
11:30 AM							
11:45 AM							
12:00 PM							
12:15 PM							
12:30 PM							
12:45 PM							
1:00 PM	Family time						
1:15 PM							
1:30 PM							
1:45 PM							
2:00 PM							
2:15 PM							
2:30 PM							
2:45 PM							
3:00 PM							
3:15 PM		Read					
3:30 PM							
3:45 PM							
4:00 PM		Work-related email					
4:15 PM							
4:30 PM							
4:45 PM							

5:00 PM	Make dinner	Make dinner	Organize office & create to-do list for next day				
5:15 PM							
5:30 PM			Drive home				
5:45 PM							
6:00 PM			Make dinner & family time				
6:15 PM							
6:30 PM							
6:45 PM							
7:00 PM	Tidy up	Tidy up					
7:15 PM							
7:30 PM	Read	Family time & relax					
7:45 PM							
8:00 PM							
8:15 PM							
8:30 PM			Evening prep (tidy up, lay out clothes, make lunch)				
8:45 PM							
9:00 PM	Evening prep	Evening prep	Personal time with spouse & sleep				
9:15 PM							
9:30 PM							
9:45 PM							
10:00 PM			Sleep				
10:15 PM							
10:30 PM							
10:45 PM							

11:00 PM	Sleep	Sleep					
11:15 PM							
11:30 PM							
11:45 PM							

The key to being successful with any routine is consistency. Adhere to your routine daily. The activities may change occasionally—just remain consistent. If you follow your routine, it will eventually become habitual.

Exercise Daily

Physical activity should be a very important part of your daily routine. Exercising every day doesn't mean going to the gym and going through a laborious workout. You define your exercise. It could be tidying up the apartment, washing and waxing your car, taking long walks or using the stairs instead of the elevator at work. The key is to do some form of activity daily. The experts say exercising three days a week is sufficient. I don't have a problem with that prescription, but what I've noticed over the years is that very few people can maintain a three-day a week regimen. When you plan to exercise multiple days a week, there's always something that gets in the way. Believe it or not, it's easier to do some form of exercise daily then it is to do it a few days a week consistently.

Exercise doesn't have to be unpleasant, yet so many people look upon it as a necessary evil with nothing but sweat and pain. There are many other things that people would rather be doing. If you start taking on the challenge of exercising consistently and you bring along a negative attitude then your new goal will perish after a few weeks.

Exercise is not a supplement to life—it's an integral part.

Establish a To-Do List

Use a simple process to document and prioritize your daily activities. Your to-do list should be written every evening or as the last task before leaving work. Don't wait until the start of each day to document your activities. You need to hit the ground running in the morning instead of wasting time by thinking of what to do next.

You don't have to buy a fancy organizer to be structured. Make it simple. Handwrite your tasks on an 8½" x 11" pad of paper and cross them off with a marker upon completion. Below are some helpful tips to assist you:

❏ This to-do list should be next to you or in front of you, not on your computer. You should take it with you throughout the day. Also, as you strategize (perhaps while waiting for a red light to change, or waiting for your doctor appointment), make notes about what needs to be done. The list should be written in pen or pencil, and all completed items should be crossed out with a thick marker.

❏ Prioritize your tasks.

Preparing a to-do list may sound simple but so many people have a hard time achieving this simple form of structure every day. You need to do this!

Focus on One Project at a Time

Don't multitask. Our brains can't efficiently handle several tasks in parallel. If you're waterskiing, you probably shouldn't be thinking about what you're going to eat for dinner. You need to focus on staying upright and on those skis.

The more effort you dedicate to the task at hand, the more likely you will complete it successfully and quickly. Thinking about several things or switching between them wastes valuable cycles. It takes time for you to gather the relevant information for any project. If you were a computer technician and you were working on upgrading a program, you would be reading through lines of code to determine your next move. If you were interrupted by someone else to work on another program, it would take you time to assess this code and then you would most likely have to start all over again with your initial program.

My recommendation is to stick to a schedule (see the section on Mastering Time). Dedicate an N number of resources and try to stick with it. Discourage others from interrupting (in the politically correct manner) or work in a *quiet* area if at all possible.

The one exception to this rule is when searching for work and most job ads require you to multitask—don't practice it. It's more important to let potential employers know that you focus and see tasks through to completion. If you try to take it all on (e.g., email every few minutes, talking to colleagues aimlessly, work on a project) you will surely fail. Don't look at email every few minutes—view it three times a day maximum, and perhaps in the early evening, unless your company culture requires you to look at it frequently.

Live Life by the 80/20 Rule

Sometimes you lack the knowledge, skills or consciousness to achieve your vision, goals or projects. You don't *always* have to do something perfectly or completely for it to be worthwhile; however, it should be completed on schedule. Take your project as far as you can. Then polish or complete it later. Eighty percent done is better than another missed or failed project. Individuals often get too detail-oriented on any given project—taking much longer than originally anticipated. It's important to complete projects and tasks on schedule or preferably ahead of schedule. This scenario is for a project that can't be separated into phases or smaller steps. Complete it on schedule—put a stake in the ground and complete it.

For projects that can be separated into smaller steps, establish multiple tasks—separate them into phases with each step becoming a goal. Focus on completing each goal in a quality manner and on schedule.

Accomplishments are addicting. Remember the last time you were proud of yourself for achieving something. What was your mood? Get those feelings back—over and over again!

Strategize

Always look for ways to improve. How can I accomplish my goals faster? How can I be more efficient today? How can I make more money? How can I create more services that people will want to purchase? How can I be healthier? You are programming that personal computer you carry in your head to be goal-oriented, creative, resourceful and a problem solver.

Visualize your future and how you want it to be. Doodle it out on a piece of paper. Make it real. Make it solid. The more energy you put into creating your future, the better it acts as a magnet to attract what you need.

You can create a vision board, using photos and drawings that symbolize what you want in your future.

Direction

Where are you going in different areas of your life?

❏ Be sure to visualize alternative solutions to complete your goals. Emergencies or other potentially negative events could derail your progress. Always have backup plans to complete your goals in the face of:
  - Economic downturn
  - Layoff
  - Corporate merger
  - Relocation

Alignment

Everything should support your long-term objectives.

❏ Align your actions to your values.
❏ Align your actions and daily routines to your goals.
❏ Align milestones to goals.
❏ Align your priorities and goals.

Goals

Goals can be:

❏ Things you want to do
❏ Things you want to purchase (home, car)
❏ Things you want to be
❏ Things you want to achieve
❏ Places you want to travel

Policy

The rules you use to achieve success, such as:

❏ Never give up
❏ Always be fair in business dealings
❏ Think with a sense of urgency
❏ Continuously challenge yourself
❏ Always strategize to achieve perfection

Plans

The backup tactics to ensure success.
❏ How are you going to achieve your goals?
❏ How will you handle emergencies that could derail progress?

Projects

You need to get something done that requires several steps. This is a project, such as:
❏ Building a tree house for your daughter
❏ Developing a new software program
❏ Moving your corporate offices from one location to another.

Flexibility Versus Fixed Ideas

One acquires fixed ideas, unexamined assumptions, from one's culture, family or friends. Flexibility is being able to change one's ideas as new data comes in.

Adaptability

In times of change it is easy to want to cling to the familiar. However, one needs to think out of the box and learn new technologies, face new challenges, and solve new problems.

Remain Future-Focused

What does that mean? There is a lot of talk about being in the now. Now is good, but without context, it doesn't have much meaning. You give your life context with your goals.

If you only stay in the now, you run the risk of getting lost and distracted. Your actions here and now lead into the future. Tomorrow comes.

Getting stuck on what happened in the past is not fun. If you made a mistake, understand what happened, institute a policy so it doesn't happen again and move on. Just as you got back up when you were learning to walk. If you do this, it will make the difference between success and failure.

Exercise:

You wind up being late for an appointment. You look at your usual routine that made you late and realize you have a tendency to leave things to the last minute not giving yourself any leeway. So you make a rule for yourself: Give myself extra time and then you start acting on that rule. Ask yourself: "Am I giving myself enough time or do I need more?" Do this until the rule becomes a habit.

Whether it's your career, health or a relationship continuously strategize to improve the situation.

❏ How can I complete my milestones in a more efficient manner?
❏ How can I complete that project ahead of schedule?
❏ How can I make more money?
❏ Although my department doesn't have a training budget, how can I acquire the skills I need?
❏ How can I get my foot into management?
❏ How can I get more out of my workout?
❏ How can I get more done in less time?
❏ How can I change my routine frequently so I don't get bored?
❏ How can I spend more quality time with my family?
❏ How can I communicate better with my significant other?
❏ How can we take more vacations together?

Don't just settle! Don't stop there. Continuously strategize to improve your life.

Corporate Promotion

If you're an employee there's no greater feeling then working hard and getting a pay raise or a promotion for it. Climbing the corporate ladder is a *great* feeling. It's a sense of accomplishment and can be extremely rewarding financially. Continuously strategize on how to get that corporate promotion faster. Here are some helpful tips.

❏ **Know your competition.** It's a constant battle in the corporate world. There are always several people vying for that one senior position. The better you know your competition and their mannerisms, the better prepared you will be for the battle.

❏ **Always work hard.** Never slack off. Many times the person with better work habits gets the promotion. It's not always guaranteed because in many situations it's who you know. However, it does help your odds if you are disciplined (driven, focused, energetic, goal-oriented and efficient).

❏ **Assess your strengths and weaknesses.** Evaluate your skills and invest in the appropriate training. Determine which skill sets you need now—prioritize them and make it happen.

❏ **If possible see if someone will mentor you.** This is not always possible because very few people have the extra bandwidth but it doesn't hurt to check—be able to provide them with something in return.

❏ **Maintain a positive attitude.** This goes without saying! Even if you have a "bad hair day" you can never show it. Maintain your composure at all times.

❏ **Get on senior management's radar daily.** Invest the extra effort in building appropriate relationships, working extra hours in the evenings and weekends to showcase your company dedication and loyalty.

❏ **Be patient.** Give it time—a promotion doesn't happen overnight.

Do whatever it takes to get that promotion. In this era of uncertainty, continuously challenge yourself to push smarter and harder. Be two steps ahead of your nearest competition.

Small Business

Having your own business and working hard to make it successful is extremely stimulating, and many individuals need that mental rush to thrive. If you don't have your own business, you can start one, but nothing grandiose. With the Internet there are endless possibilities, but that's easier said than done. Where do you begin? Here are a few things to consider:

❏ Which business would give you the biggest bang for the buck?

❏ Which business would excite you?

❏ Which business would capitalize on your strengths and perhaps help you develop your weaknesses?

❏ If you have several different business interests, research them thoroughly. Look at your top 3 interests:
  • Determine which one has a better opportunity to be profitable—based on market research.
  • How many similar businesses are already established?
  • Are they all successful?
  • Which one has the least competition?

- Who would your customers be? Is there a demand for your services or products?

❑ Pick the top 2 business ideas.

❑ Make a list to determine the upside and downside of each.

❑ Look at the overall investment required in time and money. There will always be a financial investment involved.

❑ Decide on one business and develop a business plan. This plan should include but not limited to:
  - Financial planning
  - Business structure
  - Location
  - Marketing plan
  - Business name
  - Licensing & permits
  - Technology requirements (security, backups, accounting)
  - Operations

Summary

In the *Step 1* section I highlighted what being structured means and how to institute it into your everyday life. Being successful starts with getting your life organized. Structure is the foundation for individuals and organizations to be successful. You can't be efficient if everything around you is in a chaotic state.

Instilling structure is hard work, especially when you're undisciplined. For some people it could take weeks or even months—due to the years of neglect. I had one client take more than nine months to organize his apartment, paperwork, email, and work environment. The effort was enormous. He actually had to hire a temporary administrative assistant to file his paperwork. Although it was laborious, the rewards were second to none.

There's more to instituting structure in your life than being organized. Below is a more comprehensive list of areas to address.

❑ Establish a daily routine that embraces your priorities.

❑ Treat every day equally by following your routine and focusing on your milestones first.

❑ Do some form of exercise daily.

❑ Establish a to-do list every evening.
  - Work on your brain-intensive activities in the morning—not in the afternoon when you're typically tired (especially

after lunch).
- Focus on one project at a time.
- Create a to-do list seven days a week. All tasks and obligations should be noted (personal and professional).
- Maintain it throughout the day (cross things off as soon as you complete them).

❏ Continuously strategize to look for ways to complete your goals expeditiously and improve the quality of your life.

In the corporate world structure is many things (e.g., policies, procedures, clearly defined roles and responsibilities). It's one of the greatest feelings in the world to be structured in every aspect of your personal and professional life: you can locate any document easily, save time in the morning by laying out your work clothes the night before and facilitate meetings that follow an agenda. If your life is structured you'll be able to strategize and focus on the big-ticket items (e.g., home, career) effectively. However, the key is personal buy-in. Make the commitment to get structured and you have taken the first step on the path to being disciplined.

Once you're structured, don't just set goals without prioritizing your life first. In the next section (Step 2), I educate you on what priorities are and which ones are the most critical for success.

STEP 2: PRIORITIZE YOUR LIFE

Life is hectic, demanding and stressful at times. Trying to manage your career, family obligations, friends, daily errands, and home without prioritizing your life is futile. The odds of success are greatly improved if you do things in a well-planned, structured and prioritized manner. Unfortunately, most people do not stop to think about the benefits of prioritizing and do not know how to successfully do so.

As I traveled the world and spoke on the subject of success, I would ask the audience a very simple question: "Do you prioritize your life?" If the answer is yes then I ask: "What are your priorities?" Some of the most popular answers are:

❏ To be happy
❏ To be successful
❏ To be in a wonderful relationship
❏ To be healthy
❏ To be financially set

These are great goals. All of us want to be happy and successful. However, they're not priorities. Priorities are the areas you focus on to help you accomplish your goals. Take a major league sports franchise (e.g., NFL, NBA or MLB) for example. The goal for any team is to win the championship. Successful franchises strategize and develop a roadmap with a *prioritized* list of milestones to help them achieve that goal. They would:

❏ Evaluate results from the previous year (what worked and what didn't work).
❏ Assess strengths and weaknesses in every position.
❏ Conduct a gap analysis (Do you have the right players with the right skills in the right positions?).
❏ *Prioritize* positions.
❏ Do background checks (family, lifestyle, GPA) on potential players.
❏ Recruit from the college draft or free agency based on these *priorities*.

These businesses know they can't fill all of their needs in one year—they have no choice but to *prioritize* and develop a plan. In life, individuals can't have everything they want all at one time either. If they try (and many do), they typically fail.

The priorities I recommend for individuals (90% of the time) are *career, health* and *relationships* or, as I commonly call them, *the big three*. Focusing on *the big three* will have you living a very rewarding life. Below is a process flow on how to prioritize your life.

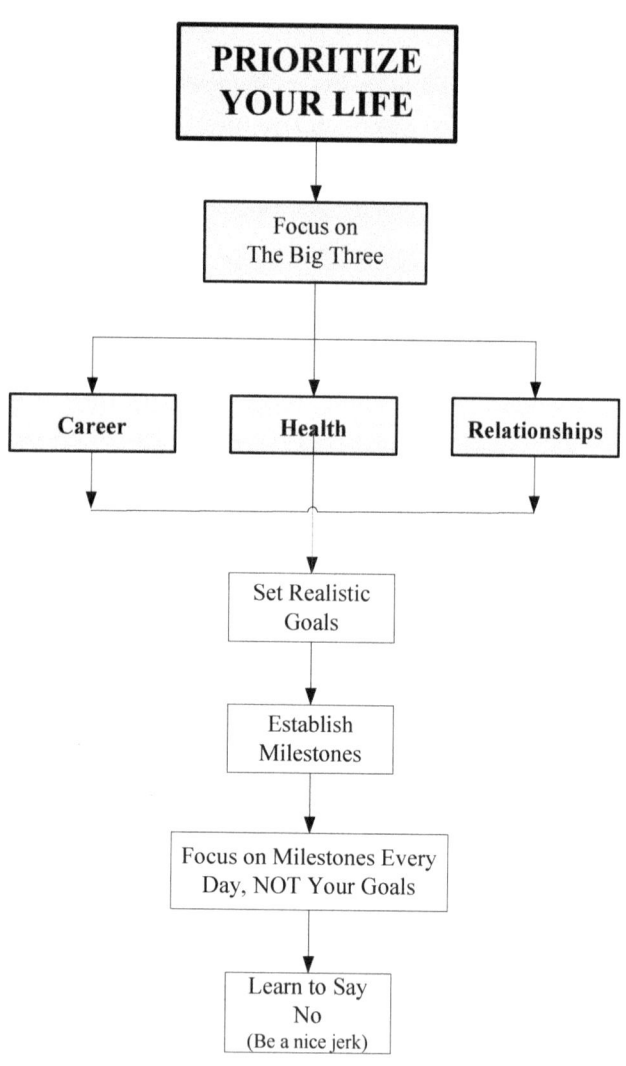

Focus on the Big Three

The three most critical priorities to focus on for success are:

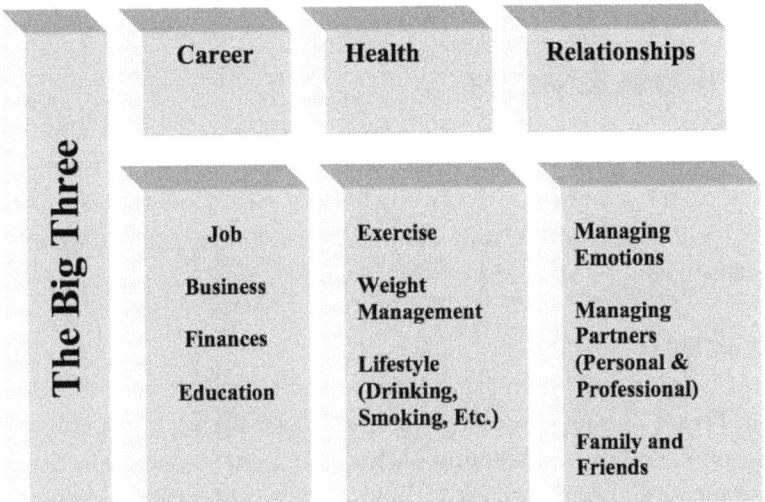

To achieve great results in your personal and professional life, focus on these three priorities. Why can't it be more? My past experiences working with organizations and individuals for several decades indicate that four is too many and will clutter your mind with too much to think about. This will make you actually less productive. Your brain can only handle so much data at one time— it starts slowing down and takes longer to process things. However, two is not enough to challenge you sufficiently.

However, these three priorities can be seen as two. I consider *career* and *health* as #1. They are interchangeable. You can't be successful without focusing on both of these. A close second or a third number one priority is relationships. If you're not proactive and manage professional and personal relationships, they will come back and cause havoc.

Set Realistic Goals

Establish goals that are aligned with your priorities and have realistic due dates. Be conservative in the beginning. If you take on too much, you will fail. Once you're structured and develop your self-discipline skills, you can gradually take on more.

To achieve your goals, think "*me,*" not "*we.*" At this point in your development you don't have an abundance of resources for "*we.*" You're still inefficient. Once you master time and achieve your goals consistently, you can allocate resources to spend more time with friends or to help others.

Establish Milestones

Milestones are those small steps you take that will help you achieve your goals. For example, if your goal is to lose fifty pounds, what do you need to do every day to help you achieve that goal? If you focus on executing your daily milestones, the goals take care of themselves.

Learn to Say No

If you try to help everyone and take on too much, you will surely fail. People can offer such distractions as irrelevant conversations, personal drama or obsession with detail. Don't waste your scarce resources on individuals that can't help you accomplish your goals.

❏ **Learn to be a nice jerk.** Cut detail-oriented people off politely. Help them get to the point faster. Constantly interrupt them in a nice way.
  • Learn to tell *little white lies*. Make excuses (e.g., your boss unexpectedly announced a mandatory meeting).
  • Don't have lengthy conversations with colleagues (e.g., in the hallway, break room), unless it benefits your career— then by all means, schmooze with them.

Priorities Versus Goals

The formal definition of *priority* is: precedence, especially established by order of importance or urgency.

Priorities are life-altering. Everything you do going forward should be aligned with these priorities.

The definition of a *goal* is the purpose toward which an endeavor is directed, an objective. All your goals need to be aligned with your priorities. Goals are the building blocks within a priority. The only way to ensure that your goals receive the attention they deserve is to focus on your priorities 24-7-365. In turn, you will be maximizing the time and resources available to achieve your goals. Individuals make the mistake of setting goals without prioritizing their lives. That is a perfect formula for failure.

There is much more to life than career, health and relationships; however, everything else should be placed in the bonus category, to be accomplished once your daily obligations and milestones have been achieved.

Simplify Your Priorities

The more complicated your life is, the more difficult it is to focus. When things are cumbersome and chaotic, our brain wants to shut down. The same goes with priorities. As an exercise I would ask my clients to categorize and prioritize their life.

"Bill" (not his real name) was a thirty-seven-year-old married man earning approximately 40K a year. He had no children. His major goals were to earn more money and be consistent managing his overall health (exercise daily and maintain good eating habits). He also wanted to maintain a good personal life with his family, wife and friends.

Bill was very ambitious and had established many goals. He was also a self-help junkie. He would buy just about every self-help book that was published, listen to dozens of CDs and attend endless seminars on success—this has been going on for years until he met me. We immediately put an end to purchasing self-help propaganda. It was time to put his knowledge to work and execute.

Bill's major challenges were lousy time management and poor goal management. He wasted an enormous amount of time and set unrealistic goals without prioritizing his life, he also couldn't hold himself accountable.

I coached Bill for about a year to resolve the issues. One of the first things we did was to simplify his priorities. His initial list had six different priorities to think about (see below).

Career / Business
❏ Real estate investment / Property ownership
❏ Music
❏ 9-to-5 job in property management

Health
❏ Weight lifting
❏ Cardiovascular
❏ Diet

Relationships
❏ Romantic / Wife
❏ Family
❏ Friends / Social life

Recreation (Outlets)
❏ Travel / Mexico
❏ Motorcycle riding
❏ Fishing / Boating / Swimming

Personal Development
❏ Education
❏ Real estate license renewal
❏ Certified property manager (CPM) certification
❏ Leadership / Management training / Communication skills
❏ Real estate investment analysis
❏ Language education

Finances
❏ Financial net worth
❏ Savings for real estate
❏ Assets / Real estate
❏ Emergency savings
❏ Retirement
❏ Vacation savings
❏ Vacation assets
❏ Debts
❏ Student loan
❏ Charity

Below is the simplified version with his three priorities and a bonus.

1. Money
- ❏ Real Estate investment / Property ownership
- ❏ Music production
- ❏ Property management (9 to 5 job)
  - Skills development
  - Real estate license renewal
  - Certified property manager (CPM) certification
  - Leadership / Management training / Communication skills
  - Real estate investment analysis
- ❏ Finances
  - Financial net worth
  - Savings for real estate
  - Assets / Real estate
  - Emergency savings
  - Retirement
  - Debts (student loans, credit cards)
  - Charity
  - Vacation assets
  - Savings

2. Health
- ❏ Weight management
- ❏ Daily exercise

3. Relationships
- ❏ Romantic /Wife
- ❏ Family
- ❏ Friends / Social life

Bonus—Recreation (Bonus-Outlets)
- ❏ Travel / Mexico
- ❏ Motorcycle riding
- ❏ Fishing / Boating / Swimming

His life now revolved around three priorities. *Money* includes career, business, skills development, and finances. *Money* was chosen because all of his top activities involved making more money. *Health* included a good diet and exercise. *Relationship* included wife, family and friends. The bonus category was his reward when he accomplished his milestones on any given day. It's much easier to remember three priorities plus a bonus category then it is to clutter your brain. You have enough going on every day without introducing more chaos.

Career, Health, and Relationships Come First

Your career consumes at least a third of your life, which includes commuting time and the time spent on your mobile device when you're away from the office. For those individuals who own a business, it consumes much more than a third—especially for startups.

Most of us need stimulation. Our minds and bodies need to be challenged. Your career and health is the logical place to get that stimulation. When your career is challenging and stimulating you're motivated to excel in other areas of your life. When you're in great shape and routinely exercise you feel energized and motivated. You're typically more enthusiastic about life in general. Not only do you benefit from this mental stimulation, but your family or significant other can see the excitement in your life. Your career, health and relationships encompass many large goals:

- ❏ A promotion
- ❏ Shifting from being one of the team to the head of the team
- ❏ A college degree
- ❏ Being physically fit
- ❏ Having a muscular physique
- ❏ Being able to run a marathon
- ❏ Having a great marriage
- ❏ There is no greater feeling then accomplishing large goals. What a rush!

Finances

My top priority throughout my life has been sound financial management. I earn, invest, save and am frugal with expenditures. It's important to have enough money to live comfortably. Having money makes life much more enjoyable because it buys you the

freedom to go wherever you want or do whatever your heart pleases:
- ❏ Travel the world.
- ❏ Buy that dream home.
- ❏ Purchase that expensive sports car or just a good reliable car.
- ❏ Give more money to charity.

Effectively managing finances is crucial to living a good life. Being debt free, having the resources to do the things you've always wanted to do and maintaining a good relationship. More marriages break up due to financial issues than any other reason. Be proactive—don't let this happen to you.

Many people don't manage finances effectively and suffer the consequences later. Individuals do not establish any sort of budget, which typically means they don't know how much they actually spend—then they get into credit card debt and don't even realize that they spend more than they make. Having financial difficulties could derail progress in every facet of your life.

Be smart about finances. Make good financial management practices a priority. Develop a budget, track your expenses and grow your savings account.

More than Money

Although managing your finances effectively is critical and should get top billing, it's not everything. I have money, but it doesn't completely fulfill my life. Sure it's nice to have and we all need it, better than a flush bank account to feel fulfilled. Some of my greatest satisfaction derives from accomplishing a major goal. *Achievement* stays with you for life. I still remember each of my minor and major goals I accomplished in my teens and twenties. Till this day each one of those accomplishments puts a smile on my face.

> "The best things in life aren't things."
> Art Buchwald

It's all about *accomplishments!* That's what really turns me on. Why bother living or just plain old existing if you did the same old boring thing every day of your life. There's no greater feeling in the world than successfully accomplishing that major goal that you've invested years of your life into.

Health

To effectively accomplish any goal you must be in good health. Your mind needs your body in perfect condition. By *perfect* I mean the best condition that you are able to attain given your circumstances. Without your body in the best possible condition you will be adding another obstacle on your road to success. Your body and mind need to work as one.

Exercise an Extension of Your Career

I'm too busy at work—there's never enough time to exercise...

For most people their job, career or business receive top priority and rightly so—especially with this economically challenged global marketplace. In the era of *doing more with less* many of you are working ten-plus hours a day plus weekends just to keep up. Some days you feel fine—some days you do not. For those of you who want to exercise consistently it's very challenging especially trying to go after work. You might have:

❏ Family obligations.
❏ Projects with unrealistic deadlines which keep you at work.
❏ Errands to run.
❏ Dinner appointments, etc...

Not to mention gyms are typically packed with people during primetime after-work hours. Your odds of accomplishing your health-related goals aren't very good.

Train your mind to believe that your workday starts 30 minutes prior to your actual start time. If you typically start work at nine each morning make yourself believe that work actually starts at eight-thirty. Use that extra half hour to exercise, even if it's just a brisk walk. Health is part of your career, without it there is no career. One may argue that health comes before career. You need to focus on both areas to have a rewarding, productive and most importantly a healthy life. There is no bargaining chip here—you need to exercise consistently—PERIOD!

Exercise in the Morning

Exercise wakes up your metabolism. How long does it take for you to be alert when you arrive at work? A couple cups of coffee? How much productivity is wasted each day thirty minutes? An hour? How many hours for the week? How many days are wasted throughout the year? When you exercise before you begin work you're already alert when you get to the office. The wheels in your brain are already turning at a high RPM for hours. Additional benefits include:

- ❏ **Gives you a positive outlook all day long.** You feel great. Your demeanor is positive. There's no better way to start the day!
- ❏ **Improves the quality of your sleep.** You'll definitely sleep better at night. If you had problems sleeping previously—waking up earlier to exercise should remedy that. You should also have less problems falling asleep.
- ❏ **You're more creative and resourceful.** You're typically more creative when you're well rested, stimulated and energized.
- ❏ **Your productivity will increase.** It's easier to remain consistent when you make exercise your first major activity of the day. With consistent exercise comes a higher level of energy and stamina, therefore productivity will increase.
- ❏ **Regulates your appetite for the rest of the day.** You eat less because since activity causes the release of endorphins, which diminish your appetite. Another bonus is that you typically eat healthier foods.
- ❏ **Increases mental acuity.** Studies have shown that exercising significantly increases mental acuity—a benefit that lasts four to ten hours. Exercising before going to work means utilizing that extra brainpower when it's mostly needed—not wasting it while you're sleeping because you worked out in the evening.

Relationships

Your resources are scarce and once you complete your milestones, there are very little left over for anything else. Then there is your family—they need to get top billing. Who has time to build relationships? Typically nurturing key business relationships is taken for granted and put on the back burner.

The first step is to realize that you need to pick and choose relationships most critical for your success. I recommend building solid relationships with:

❏ Your significant other
❏ Key executives/colleagues in the corporate world who can enhance your career
❏ Your business partner
❏ God

What about friends? If you have the time, then by all means— but unfortunately there are very little to no cycles left in this scenario. That's just reality. Don't forget family: they're above all of this and *always* demand your attention.

Your Significant Other

We have entered into relationships since the Stone Age. What we have not been able to accomplish yet is to maintain healthy strong relationships. What exactly is a strong relationship? One in which two people work together toward a common goal. It is not abusive in any manner. It is communicating and coming to a common compromise; there are no winners because you worked together. So what does it take to build that strong relationship? Below are some helpful tips.

1. **Trust.** Trust is everything. Without trust there will be no relationship. You can have a shell of a relationship, but nothing will truly be there. Think about all the people you know that question their spouse about every little detail of the day. Trust is vital for any relationship to become strong and everlasting.

2. **Honesty.** Where does a relationship go without honesty? No one truly wants a relationship based on lies. Even white lies will eventually turn into great big lies that forever need to be covered up. Be honest with your spouse at all costs. Lies are like a poisonous gas that will silently kill your relationship.

3. **Time spent together.** Sounds easy, right? Think again. With the hustle and bustle all around us it is extremely hard to make time for anyone in your life. Sometimes you have a tendency to forget that the other person is there. Do not let this happen to you. Always make time to spend with that special person in your life.

4. **Forgiveness.** Forgiveness is essential for a strong relationship. Now, I am not saying to forgive unfaithfulness. What I am saying is to learn to forgive your mate's harsh or offensive words every now and then. Sometimes we get into moods and say things we really don't mean. As long as this doesn't happen daily or even weekly, take the time to find it in your heart to forgive your mate.

5. **Agreement to disagree.** Disagreements will happen. Avoid fighting; it only fuels the fire and we always end up saying something that we really don't mean. Hurtful things happen when we fight; stay as far away from that as possible. Not every couple is going to agree on everything. Successful couples agree to disagree. If it is not a life-threatening matter, just let it go.

6. **Compromise.** Ah, where would this world be without compromise? *Nowhere.* That is exactly where your relationship will end up if you do not practice compromise.

7. **Communication.** This is a vital key to strength in your relationship. How are we to know what our spouses are thinking or what is going on in their lives if there is no communication? Did you know that most arguments or disagreements between couples generally stem from a lack of communication? The best way to improve communication with your spouse or significant other is to involve them in your world—especially your professional world. I manage three businesses: my wife is involved in each of them. She's aware of my activities and I often have her assist me. I also take her to the gym and take walks with her and we just talk about random stuff. It's easier to communicate when you have common interests.

8. **Listening.** Always give your spouse your full attention and really *listen*. There is nothing more annoying than talking to someone's back. Hearing is not the same as listening. Try and understand your spouse's perspective; don't react or become defensive. Relationships need such listening.

9. Lovemaking. No matter how much life gets in the way, make time for intimacy. It has been said that your sex life with your spouse directly corresponds with your success rate as a couple. It is true. When you are intimate with your spouse, be in that moment. Don't be a million miles away in your mind; turn yourself over completely to the intimacy.

After you've established a strong relationship, proactively manage it. Just because things are okay right now doesn't mean they will remain that way. Things can change suddenly and cost you countless days of lost productivity. The most important area to focus on is communication.

Over-Communicate

Lack of communication is a huge issue in relationships, especially in this era of trying to do more with less. Who has the time to have meaningful and constructive conversations? You do. You have no choice—do it! Below are several tips on how to effectively communicate with your significant other.

- ❏ **Schedule a date night once a week and/or couple time nightly.** Whether it's ten minutes, or thirty minutes, find a time of night to talk—with the TV off.
- ❏ **Never go to sleep during a heated argument.** Make every possible effort to resolve it. Don't let it drag on for days or weeks.
- ❏ **Learn to give in.** Don't be stubborn. Learn to say *I am sorry*—even if it's not your fault. It doesn't matter who's to blame. You have too many other things to worry about.
- ❏ **Try to listen to your partner.** Don't interrupt, even if it's a heated discussion and even if the discussion is baseless and doesn't make any sense. Let them get it all out—and pay attention to *what* they're saying instead of *how* they're saying it.
- ❏ **Don't bring up past negative incidents.** Things that happened in the past are irrelevant. They will only make things worse.
- ❏ **Choose your words carefully.** You never know when a certain word could be taken the wrong way—don't take a chance of being misunderstood. Sometimes a normal

discussion of a sensitive issue can get ugly quickly. Just like you choose your words carefully in the corporate world there is no difference here—be politically astute!

❏ **Be respectful at all times.** Don't mock or belittle. Listen conscientiously and value their opinion. Be kind, soft-spoken and well-mannered.

❏ **Find a quiet place to have discussions.** No TV or loud noise.

❏ **Before discussing a sensitive issue—don't just blurt out the problem—provide a solution first.** For example, don't just tell your partner that they never cook dinner. Suggest, instead, that you schedule a time to cook.

❏ **Winning an argument is irrelevant**. Don't go there.

❏ **Respect your partner at all times.** Treat your partner as you wish to be treated. No name-calling, no sarcasm, no teasing—always highlight their strengths.

❏ **Always be honest.** Lies beget lies.

❏ **Don't cause a disturbance by yelling, throwing something, hitting something or storming out of a room and slamming a door.** This type of behavior will only exacerbate a negative situation. Don't make a scene. Exercise to release tension and become calm.

❏ **It takes two to tango.** Don't blame each other. It takes both of you to argue. Look for common ground—learn to give in. Look for positive scenarios.

Bring Them into Your World

I know it's difficult to keep your significant other abreast of your work activities, especially on a regular basis. Make every attempt to summarize what's going on. Don't exclude them. Treat them like your business partner. Remember: they're your life partner.

If one of you is managing the finances for the household, update your spouse. Share a formal document on a spreadsheet, which you can both review together. You should review the status of your finances at least monthly. While reviewing your finances together, discuss goals, milestones, priorities and vacations. Bond as partners.

Be proactive with your partner for personal and professional issues. After living with someone for a long time, most of us take good communication practices for granted—especially for what we may consider to be an insignificant issue. It might be a sore spot for your partner. Whether it's keeping your personal life in harmony by proactively communicating or networking with key executives to improve your stature in the workplace, communication is the key ingredient for success.

Schmoozing with Key Executives and Colleagues

My wife commonly refers to schmoozing as kissing butt. Well, schmoozing is how you network. It also plays a big role in marketing and sales, getting deals done, developing and maintaining long-term relationships with customers, garnering support from your peers and co-workers, selling your ideas and even getting ahead in your career.

My wife struggled in her management career because she failed to schmooze with the appropriate people. As she put it, "I'm not about to kiss anyone's butt." I told her that schmoozing was not about kissing someone's butt. In fact, the definition of *schmooze* is "to converse informally, to chat, or to chat in a friendly and persuasive manner especially so as to gain favor, business or connections." Who among you doesn't consider that to be a critical part of business success? Below are ten tips to help you build strong relationships and business connections through the art of schmoozing.

1. **Don't BS.** Let's get one thing straight. BSing destroys credibility. If you want to become a successful executive or leader, don't BS. Period. It doesn't matter how smart others think you are, just how smart you really are.

2. **It's never about you—it's always about them.** Connecting with people means finding things you have in common, or even different views on a subject you both feel strongly about. You already know you: what you don't know is *them*.

3. **People like to be schmoozed.** People like attention, to be noticed, to connect and engage. That is, as long as you're straightforward about it.

4. **Be open and genuine.** Be you. The most effective way to connect with people and find common ground is to be yourself, with all your native charm, faults, and idiosyncrasies. There's nothing more attractive than being yourself.

5. **Don't overdo it.** Next to BSing and trying to be someone you're not, *trying too hard* is the biggest schmoozing pitfall. Pushing too hard will backfire.

6. **Everyone is schmoozable.** CEOs, VPs, tough administrative assistants: everyone is schmoozable, for the simple reason that everyone likes the attention—under the right conditions.

7. **Always be appropriate.** Never overstep your bounds or make others feel uncomfortable. Never invade someone's personal space. Not sure what the boundaries are? It's different for everyone, so pay attention: they'll let you know.

8. **Always be respectful of people's time.** Now more than ever, our time is our most precious resource.

9. **Don't talk at people.** Nobody likes to be talked *at*. They like to be engaged. They like to be listened to. There's a big difference. Just remember: give a little, get a little.

10. **Let yourself be schmoozed.** Although, by definition, schmoozing is related to persuasion, you'll be better off just thinking of it in terms of long-term relationships. That means you should always be willing to help people first. It's good karma.

Make Time to Network

There's not enough time to build relationships with everyone. You need to pick and choose the relationships that can most benefit you. Forge relationships with professionals who can persuade others to help you get ahead. Professionals that can help you get that promotion or get that big bonus. Promotions and larger bonuses aren't necessarily given to those who work the hardest or produce the greatest results. Bonuses and promotions are often awarded to the people who you least expect. They often received it because of *who* they know.

Unfortunately, to do this right takes a *large* investment of time. Whether it's a lunch meeting, impromptu discussions in the hallway, or a golf excursion. Below are a few additional tips on how to effectively schmooze, given the time constraints you face in life.

❑ **Design a strategy with a detailed roadmap.** Identify the key individuals you need to schmooze with:
  • Prioritize the list.
  • Determine what key points you want the individual to know about you. Make a mental list and drop them into a conversation at the appropriate time—but only one at a time. Less is better in the beginning. Don't bombard this person with a lot of data about yourself. Compliment them first. Tell them you've admired their work for the longest time.
  • Find out through friends or colleagues what someone likes. Let's say they like baseball—occasionally peruse ESPN. com to look at the headlines to strike up a conversation.

❑ **Flatter them.** Use flattery to establish key relationships. *How did you turn that customer around? We were about to lose our largest source of income. I'd love to learn your secrets.*

❑ **Ask your boss for his or her opinion.** It's a great way to begin a relationship. Executives love it when their subordinates ask them questions. It can make them come away from a conversation with a more favorable impression of you. Most executives have egos—they love to talk about themselves or just hear themselves speak. Don't just ask questions about work. Branch out and ask about their weekend plans, family or church.

❑ **Come in the back door.** Don't always agree immediately. Yield before accepting your manager's opinion. Try something like this: "At first I didn't agree with your statement, but now that I've had a chance to reflect it makes perfect sense to me."

❑ **Talk as if you belong.** Be respectful, but speak as though you're on the same professional level. Don't be negative or complain about your job or your personal life, a bureaucratic process or an issue with a co-worker. Never complain or share too much information to management—they have a short attention span. If you feel like you must complain, bring a solution to the discussion.

Business Partner

The first cardinal rule to picking a business partner: make sure you know the person. Assess his or her strengths and weaknesses.

You want a partner that actually helps you strengthen your weaknesses. But you also want a partner that's driven, resourceful, creative, committed to the business and in possession of a sense of urgency. It helps if he or she is a good communicator and has a good personality. Below are a few simple tips on how to choose the right business partner.

- ❏ Do not pick a partner because he or she's a friend or a family member; pick someone because of his or her skill sets. Ideally you want someone with good self-discipline skills, a good leader, excellent EQ skills, honesty and integrity.
- ❏ When establishing a business partnership make sure you have a legal agreement—seek counsel for advice. You never know when things could go sour.
- ❏ Make sure you and your potential partner have an agreed-upon vision.
- ❏ Financial habits are important—get to know how he or she thinks financially.

Make sure you can trust your partner.

Probably the most critical aspect is to make sure you can easily communicate with your partner. After all, it's similar to a marriage, and if you can't properly communicate with your partner, the partnership will be doomed before it sees its first complete year.

Manage Conversations

There will be many unplanned disruptions throughout any given period. One of the most time-consuming interruptions is conversing with others. Many individuals have a tendency to drag conversations on. You need to know how to effectively truncate conversations. Don't be rude, but learn how to respectfully and tactfully cut them off. The balloons below provide a few suggestions for effectively managing conversations.

It's very important to clarify the difference between lying and doing whatever it takes to focus all of your precious cycles on your goals and long-term objectives. The examples above pertain to an individual's personal life, but it's no different for work-related goals. Learning to say *no* in the politically correct manner is critical for success.

This conversation is too important to discuss in a few minutes. It definitely warrants more time. Do you mind if we schedule sometime next week?

I wish I had more time to discuss this particular item with you, but I'll be late for work. Let's schedule sometime in the next few weeks to talk further.

Your explanation is right on the mark. I will give it some serious thought and get back to you when I'm not so pressed for time.

As much as I want to continue this subject I need to run an errand for my parents before the store closes. Can we talk later?

I love this conversation and would love to continue it, but I'm sorry I have an appointment. Perhaps we can talk another time?

Effectively Managing Professional Conversations

Management has asked me to work on some very critical projects. I'd love to meet with your customer, but can it please wait until next month?

Thank you for calling and bringing your request to my attention. My schedule has been hectic lately and the number of requests has been growing exponentially. Do you mind if we schedule some time tomorrow to review this issue?

I truly would love to help you out, but can I please get back to you as soon as I can, maybe in the next 2 to 4 weeks? My travel schedule has been overwhelming and I really need to spend some time with my family.

My workload is overwhelming right now and I truly understand the urgency with your request. However I would hate to default on my previous commitments. Do you mind if I ask my manager for guidance? Perhaps he can assign someone to help out.

Learn to Say No

Learn to say no with grace. Some of these methods may not seem appropriate, but utilizing scarce resources to their fullest sometimes requires being resolute.

So often we give more value to others wishes and priorities than to our own. The idea is to learn balance.

Balance means a satisfying arrangement of parts. It is equilibrium between two opposing forces. There are the demands put on you by work and family, church and groups. Then there are self-imposed demands. Your priorities have a force of their own. It is useful to learn how to balance out the demands. Below are additional examples of how to manage conversations (in the politically correct manner) or what I refer to as being a nice jerk in somewhat difficult situations.

Scenario #1: Impromptu Discussions

How many times do you walk the hallways at work and have someone stop you to chitchat? If you add up the minutes wasted from these impromptu meetings it would be truly eye-opening. If these discussions do not pertain to your job function, then cut them off. It's very simple: "Excuse me, Ted, I would love to speak with you right now but I have an urgent matter to address back at my desk. Please let's catch up next week."

Of course by next week, something else will come up—Ted will eventually get the hint. It's as simple as that! Your time is too valuable. This doesn't mean not to schmooze or network! It does mean managing your time effectively and connecting with the people who can help you in your career. You have no choice but to be selective.

Scenario #2: Slow Talker

Speed slow talkers along. People who are detail-oriented take forever to get to the point. Don't waste your time by listening to every syllable of every word. Speed up an individual's slow conversation without being rude. You can pretty much anticipate what their point is. Start interrupting with the potential answer in a very nice way. Just come out and say it. If it's wrong, it will force them to blurt out the correct answer, and you won't have to hear the painstaking details. I do it constantly and no one gets upset.

These people often feel they are not being heard or do not fully have your attention. Listen fully, completely. Notice the end of a paragraph and really let them know you heard them. If the person you are listening to is upset about somebody being rude, you can acknowledge them in a way that makes them feel understood. "You felt really ignored in that situation? I see that would be really upsetting."

Setting Goals

Just about everybody has set goals in one form or another, but how many people are actually successful at accomplishing those goals? That's an easy one to answer: very few! I think everyone realizes how important it is to establish goals, but why is it that most of us fail trying to accomplish them? There are three reasons.

First, most people do not live by a mental contract. The contract sets you up with a framework for meeting goals, making it easier for you to avoid distractions and staying focused.

Second, most people do not take the time to think through their goals thoroughly. You should not just make them up after a few drinks at a New Year's Eve party.

Third, people fail because they set goals that are outlandish and impossible to accomplish. Keep within your boundaries and make sure you set goals that are realistic. Most people make the mistake of comparing themselves to a movie star or famous athlete. This virtually guarantees failure.

Think of goals this way:

❏ How long will it take to accomplish it?
❏ What will I have to sacrifice?
❏ What other areas of my life will this impact?
❏ Do I have a prayer of ever accomplishing this?

You can change a goal, but you should seek an equal or greater challenge. There can be no slacking off or lounging around. That is not the way it works. Those are the rules. So, before committing yourself, think hard. I am not talking about a few hours of daydreaming; I am referring to some real soul-searching.

Let us say you have established ten goals. There could be two or three that need adjustment over time. You should not change them all. Those that need changing should be changed once. The ideal scenario is not to change any of them; however, that is almost impossible. Things change, and you will need to adapt. You can always keep adding goals throughout this process, but you cannot remove one without replacing it.

You should never set goals that depend on someone else. Do not take this the wrong way: you still need your friends and colleagues in life, but you cannot use them to accomplish goals. There are no partnerships here. Placing dependencies on goals will surely lead to failure. You must own the goal. Sure, it is a lot of weight to carry on your shoulders, but if something goes wrong, there is no one else to blame. You cannot control or manage the actions of others.

I established some aggressive goals at a very young age. Aggressive is putting it mildly—how about outrageous! Why did I go overboard? What made me different from other young teens? I blame it on my neighbor, Jim, the man who taught me to exercise properly develop my self-discipline skills, and most importantly gave me a huge dose of self-confidence.

Jim gave me one of the greatest gifts in life: the knowledge and the mentoring to acquire discipline. He taught me to *never* miss a goal. A key component to this is having a backup plan for each goal to prevent failure.

Backup Plans

There should be more than one way to achieve a goal. In fact, you should have several. Always keep those wheels in motion by thinking of smarter and easier ways to complete goals ahead of schedule. Set milestones and challenge yourself to finish ahead of schedule. One of my goals was to be promoted once every two years—after I got a job in the corporate world at the age of eighteen. To ensure successful completion I had plenty of backup (milestones and tasks to help secure that promotion) to help me achieve my goal:

1. Complete all projects that were established by management ahead of schedule.
2. Design and complete at least two new high-visibility projects outside the scope of my current job responsibilities.
3. Continuously invest extra effort and time to assist other areas of the organization.
4. Meet with management on a quarterly basis to track progress.
5. Proactively look for ways to improve productivity and reduce costs in the organization.
6. Communicate effectively throughout the organization.
7. Network (schmooze) with key professionals.

In most instances, people would be content with completing goals set by management ahead of schedule. But, as I learned, that does not always guarantee successful completion of the overall goal. I always wanted to improve my odds.

Choose Your Own Path

Of course, there is no reason you should choose goals similar to the ones I chose. I chose mine because I had two major objectives: one was to change my physical appearance, and the other was to excel in my career. I had many minor goals along the way as well.

What are your major goals—the ones that you will accomplish over the long term? Before you decide, think long and hard and ask yourself these key questions:

1. What am I good at?
2. What do I like to do?
3. Is it aligned with my priorities?

These three questions, more than anything else, will help you in setting major goals that are right for you—goals that you will want to accomplish, and that you will accomplish successfully!

Do not establish a goal that is not aligned with your priorities. Being aligned means focusing and executing those daily milestones that help you achieve your overall objectives. For example, if one of your objectives (priorities) is a successful career, then make sure your goals and milestones will help you achieve this objective. For example:

❏ Priority = Career
❏ Goal = Learn a new job function in six months.
❏ Milestone = Read thirty minutes per day to learn about the new job function.

It is important to choose something you really like doing. Honestly assess what you're good at. This is not an easy thing for you to judge yourself. Some people, for example, think they have great talent as singers, actors, musicians or artists. Some of these people really are artists and should follow their dreams. And there are the others—those who insist on singing, playing, or painting, and you have to be polite and say nice things even though it's obvious that they have no talent. Maybe they can fulfill their fantasies in church choirs or painting as a hobby. If you're not sure of your strengths, as someone who knows you well to provide an honest assessment. Most of us tend to be blinded to our own shortcomings. We don't see ourselves as others see us.

There is a reason why many progressive companies make

everyone go through so-called 360-degree reviews: you get feedback from everyone—your boss, your peers and those who report to you—on your strengths and weaknesses. Although it might be nerve-wracking and stomach-turning to look carefully at this feedback, you owe it to yourself to do so.

If you are not lucky enough to get this type of information through a formal process, then you have no choice but to ask people yourself. Take it seriously. Make it an occasion for putting the world on notice that you are taking control of your life, setting it on a path towards success.

Tracking Goals

Once you establish goals, you need to track your progress. Performance tracking should become part of your routine.

At work, your supervisor will outline goals for the upcoming year. As an employee, your next raise or promotion will depend on how well you accomplish those goals. The same holds for personal goals.

If you only occasionally think about your goals, maybe once a week or monthly, you will surely fail. Each day you ponder about breakfast, lunch or dinner. Give your goals at least the same amount of attention. You need to focus on your goals and give them the utmost priority. If you do an incomplete job, failure will be imminent.

Goals are simple to track, but most people simply do not bother because they do not take them seriously. Then one day—surprise—the completion date for the goal is nearing quickly and you are not ready. You scramble, but it is too late.

Be persistent and consistent. It is no different from being a full–time project manager where the employer asks you to meet aggressive deadlines. That project could last three months or five years: regardless of duration, stay focused.

Major Goals vs. Minor Goals

What is the difference between major goals and minor goals? That is for you to decide. Everyone is different. You have to consider the complexity, the magnitude and your current lifestyle before deciding which goals are minor and which ones are major. Some of my minor goals could be considered major to someone else. However, remember: a goal is a goal. You must accomplish it.

Make sure goals come from the heart. You need to feel it from within. Never establish goals on impulse. In my early-to mid-twenties, I had an ego larger than the home I was living in. But now, whenever I establish a goal, it has nothing to do with ego or impulse. It comes from the heart. With continuous accomplishments comes maturity; it allows you to grow within. It is a wonderful feeling to say and believe that it truly comes from the heart. In my early twenties, I would have mocked a statement like that.

Here are the actual major goals I set at the age of thirteen:

Major Goals	Completion Date
Have 1 million dollars in assets	Age of 40
Own at least 3 homes	Age of 40
Pay cash for a luxury car (Later changed to "publish a book")	Age of 40

I actually made one drastic change to the last one of these. I was working in Silicon Valley and had become quite materialistic. It is not very hard to do in those surroundings. Hey, the more toys the better! And by the way, they had to be designer brand toys.

However, in April of 1992, on a trip to the Philippines, I gulped a dose of reality. I witnessed poor people with barely enough food to eat; yet, most of the people I met were friendly, cordial, hospitable and happy—not ecstatic about their situation, but happy. It gave me a new perspective on life. My entire life had been about money, money and more money. WOW! They were surviving without a Mercedes. I had intended to purchase the nicest Mercedes money could buy. As soon as I returned from that two-week trip, I called my car broker friend in Los Angeles—who was looking for the ultimate car for me—to cancel the order.

I wanted to change that goal. It was a risky move to change a goal, as I was nearing my fortieth birthday, but I had plenty of confidence to accomplish anything. Remember that it had to be a major goal. I decided to write and publish a book, not because of the money or fame, but for the challenge. It was completed and published by Prentice-Hall in May of 1994, one month before I turned forty.

It was a risky move, because I could have easily bought that car and paid cash for it before that trip to Manila. I'd been waiting to buy that car for over a decade; it was my personal reward for the past twenty-five years of being so disciplined. Then I decided to change it, just like that.

There was no greater personal reward than seeing my name as an author on my very first book. Especially from a kid who had barely graduated from high school—Hillsdale High, San Mateo, California. It was a remarkable feeling.

I set many more goals along the way. As you complete each goal, it makes you feel great and that much hungrier to conquer the next goal. This feeling is like no other. Completing each goal was a huge adrenaline rush. Here are *some* of the goals I set in the late sixties, seventies and eighties:

Goals	Completion Date
Deposit a minimum of $5.00 in the bank every week since the age of 13	Age of 15
Pay cash for a new car	Age of 16
Begin work in the computer industry	Age of 18 (1972)
Purchase first home	Age of 19
Purchase a boat and customize to match my car	Age of 21
Exercise daily	Ongoing
Job promotions	Minimum once every two years
Promotion to first management position	Age of 23
Pay cash for new Corvette	Age of 25
Never miss a day of work due to illness	Ongoing

Goal Management

Your daily actions add up to the final goal. It is the making of that phone call every day until you reach the person you need to speak with. It is the drilling of vocal scales that add up to expertise. It is the daily walk that adds up to increased health and endurance. It is managing these daily actions that allow you to manage your goals and it begins with developing a simple goal-setting worksheet.

The worksheet is where you document issues and problems. Next, dissect the solution into achievable and measurable action steps (milestones) to overcome that problem. Complete this exercise for both short and long-term goals. Ensure that the worksheet is reviewed daily. This should not be compromised unless there was a last-minute emergency. The following elements make up the worksheet, typically an Excel spreadsheet or Word document:

❏ **Current Problem:** All issues, obstacles, and challenges need to be documented. Certain issues and challenges can be categorized and combined into specific problem statements. For example, let's say you have the following issues:

- Abrasiveness
- Ineffective communication
- Proneness to conflict
- Inappropriate interruptions

All of these issues could be lumped under one problem statement: Poor communication practices.

❏ **Desired Results:** What do you hope to accomplish? What constitutes success? In the worksheet below, the results are to lose weight and be more energetic.

❏ **Minor and Major Goals:** Establish new major and minor goals that address specific problem statements.

❏ **Milestones:** Establish concrete milestones with due dates for each goal.

❏ **Status:** What's the status of each milestone? Are there any potential concerns or obstacles? Are there new opportunities to complete these milestones at an accelerated pace?

Current Problem: 40 pounds overweight and lack energy.		
Desired Result: Lose the weight and have more energy.		
	Due Date	Status
Goal: Improve overall health.		
Milestones:		
1. Do 30 minutes of exercise every day (walk, run, gym). Preferably in the morning before going to work or at lunch time at work (you could walk around your office park).	Ongoing	
2. Maximum of one junk food outing per week.	Ongoing	
3. Eat no more than three healthy meals per day.	Ongoing	
4. Eliminate snacking in between meals.	Ongoing	

The Hierarchy of Successful Goal Management

For each priority, establish several goals, but do not set goals that are unrealistic. Let's say that one of your goals under the priority of health is to lose fifty pounds. Once you establish goals, focus on your daily milestones. Accomplishing those small steps will eventually add up to big accomplishments. Your milestones could be:

❏ Exercise Monday, Wednesday and Friday.
❏ Reduce caloric intake on Saturday and Sunday by 25 percent.

The hierarchy for successful goal management would look like:
❏ Priorities
❏ Goals
❏ Milestones

The table below provides a snapshot of proper goal-setting.

Priority #1	Goal #1	Milestone #1
		Milestone #2
	Goal #2	Milestone #1
		Milestone #2
		Milestone #3
Priority #2	Goal #1	Milestone #1
	Goal #2	Milestone #1
		Milestone #2
	Goal #3	Milestone #1
Priority #3	Goal #1	Milestone #1

Establish Milestones for Each Goal

Let's say that your goal is to hire a new employee. This is an overwhelming task. Therefore, it is especially important to dissect this process into smaller steps. Establish milestones (smaller steps) that are conservative and realistic; don't establish milestones that are difficult to achieve. That's a recipe for failure. Here are your milestones:

1. Decide what qualities you need and what salary you are willing to pay
2. Post an ad
3. Ask questions to those in your professional network

4. Review resumes

5. Pick out the more promising ones

6. Come up with questions to ask

7. Call people in to interview

8. Review the candidates that seem the most likely fit

9. Call in for a second interview

10. Decide and inform your candidate

There are many steps involved during a recruitment process. By establishing concrete milestones you will achieve your hiring goal effectively.

Another example:

❏ Current problem—working at a job I don't enjoy and that doesn't pay well

❏ Desired result—working at a place I really enjoy and that pays well

❏ Goal—to find my dream job

The milestones for the above example are:

1. Assess whether it is the company, the sector or the type of work I'm doing

2. Determine what I really want to do

3. Start interviewing my friends who have different jobs

4. Do an analysis of my skills and see which ones are transferable

5. Research various companies I would like to work for

6. Research various sectors

7. Find out if I need to take a class to get to the next level

8. Start networking

9. Put together a resume

10. Find someone to mentor you

11. Start sending out your resume

Be prudent and very conservative when establishing milestones. Think simplicity and start small. It's important to consistently complete your milestones on schedule. Once this becomes habitual you will not miss another due date. You will get used to achieving your goals and you will be able to set and attain more difficult ones. Focusing on the goal itself may seem overwhelming at times, so chew it off in small chunks.

Summary

You can't take it all on and expect to be successful. There's those nagging errands, home chores, work, education, health-related activities, major goals and minor goals. On top of all that your family and friends need attention. How do you do it all and have some time for yourself? Prioritize your life.

Based on hundreds of individual and organizational assessments, the most important priorities are *career* (business, work, education, skills development and finances), *health* (meal management, exercise and lifestyle), and proactively managing *relationships* (with significant others, business partners, God and colleagues). Focus on these priorities and you *will* be successful.

If you don't prioritize every aspect of your life, you will fail miserably. One of the areas I had to curtail was the relationships I had with my friends. My time was very limited. I didn't have enough cycles at the end of the week to speak with my friends. But the few close friends I did have totally understood. In this section (Step 2), I also taught you how to:

❏ Simplify your priorities
❏ Establish goals that are aligned with your priorities
❏ Set goals
  • Have backup plans to ensure successful goal completion
  • Establish major and minor goals
  • Establish milestones for each goal and focus on the milestones not the goals
❏ Understand the hierarchy for successful goal management: priorities, goals and milestones
❏ Proactively manage relationships
❏ Manage conversations
  • Become a nice jerk
  • Learn to say no

Establishing priorities is easy, yet very few people take the time to do it. You have limited resources on any given day. Excelling in life starts by prioritizing it; this allows you to focus on the goals for success. Once you *institute structure* and *prioritize your life*, then and *only* then will you be able to *master time*.

STEP 3: MASTER TIME

Time is your most valuable resource. However, if you are like most people, time controls you rather than you controlling it. Did you ever stop to think why people always run out of time at the end of the day? Rarely do they get everything done on any given day. These days, time *must* be managed to get as many things done as possible in twenty-four hours.

People waste time like there's an abundance of it—they take it for granted. Most of my clients come to me with horrific time-management issues. They procrastinate until the last minute, aimlessly surfing the Internet for hours, watching too much TV, trying to pick out the clothes they want to wear first thing in the morning instead of the night before. They all see it as only a few minutes here and there. When are they going to grasp the fact that they're on this planet once and time is scarce—why not make the most of it? This section is divided into two parts: *Know Your Numbers* and *Make Every Minute Count*. Unless you know where you waste time, there's no way you can manage it effectively. On the next page is a process flow of how to effectively *master time*.

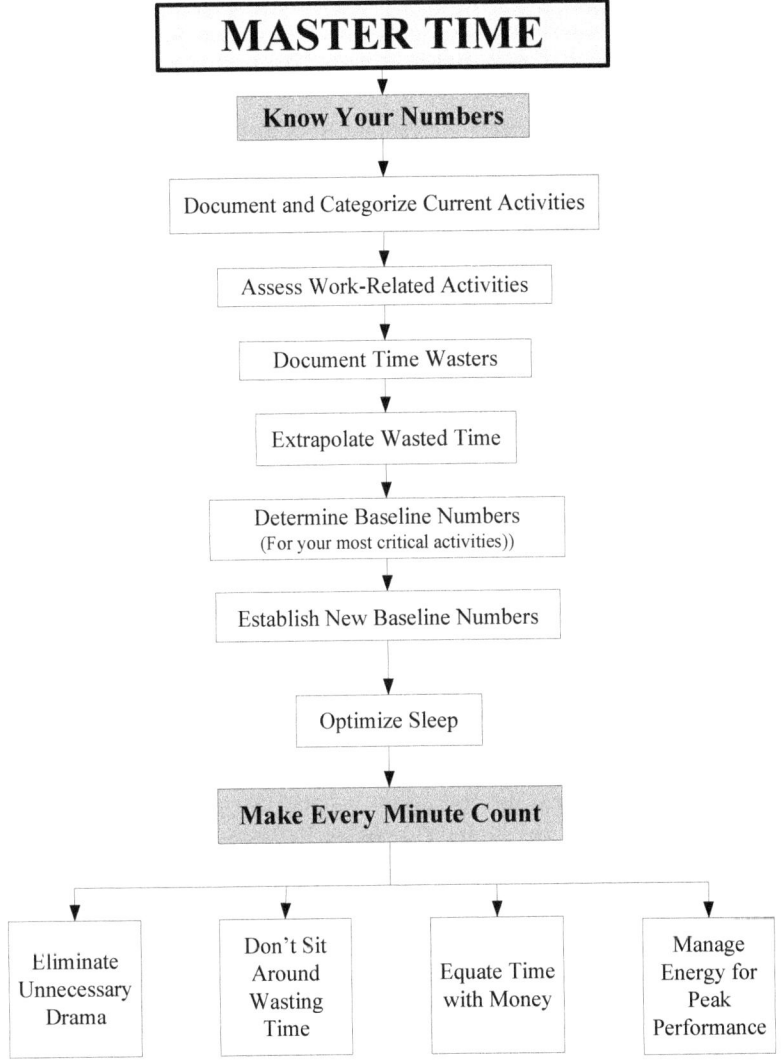

Know Your Numbers

Let's say you own a small business—your livelihood depends on its success. To be successful in business, you need a vision, strategy, goals, roadmap, processes and good people to execute. Many of your goals are financial—cash flow, sales, net profits and marketing budget. You've also established non-financial goals, such as the number of daily customers, increasing customer base and customer retention. You would constantly be looking at your numbers to assess and strategize for improvement.

Next you would break your goals into objectives that must be met to achieve success. For example, to increase your customer base, you may want to extend your business hours and improve customer service skills by offering a number of hours of training per employee. Then you may want to gauge customer satisfaction.

Would you waste time? Would you procrastinate? Of course you wouldn't—you would try to make use of every minute. You would be strategizing to be more efficient. You would constantly be looking at your numbers to see where you can do more with fewer resources.

The more you know about your business, the more effective you will be at managing it. The same is true of life; the more you know which activities are the most critical for success, and how much time is spent on each, the more successful you'll be. It's also important to know where time is being wasted. It's all about knowing your numbers.

Document and Categorize Activities

Start by documenting your current activities for one week, including the weekend. While you're documenting and categorizing your activities note the start and end time for each. Once you have your activities documented, assess where you're ineffective. Document where you waste time.

❏ How much time are you wasting watching TV?
❏ How much time do you waste trying to find things because you are disorganized?
❏ How much time is wasted chitchatting with people at work who can't help you excel in your career?

Once you know your numbers, and after picking yourself off

the floor from being shocked by those numbers, document your baseline number for success (based on your priorities):

❑ How much time are you currently devoting to improving your career?

❑ Which managers should you schmooze with?

❑ How much time are you investing to develop your work-related skills?

❑ How much time should you invest to nurture key relationships?

❑ How much time are you currently devoting to your overall health?

❑ How much should you save each week? What's the minimum amount you need to maintain in your savings account? When can you withdraw a few dollars to take a long vacation?

❑ How much should you be spending on incidentals?

If you don't know your numbers, you can't manage anything effectively. If you want to start making efficient use of your time, then you need to know where you currently stand—*assess* your daily activities. Table 3.1 below is a sample Activity Log. Included in it are columns for the Day of the week, Activity, Start Time, End Time, Total Time, Notes, Category and total Wasted Minutes. Use it as an example to create your own spreadsheet to track what you do in a day. Perform this exercise for a week. Make sure to categorize your activities. Some potential categories could be: personal time, evening prep, driving or commuting. Where is most of your time allocated? For example, let's say one of your categories is relaxation—for some reason at the end of the week you feel tired and burned out, but after looking back at your weekly activity log— you spent ten hours this week relaxing. Perhaps it's the lack of exercise that's making you sluggish. Sometimes seeing your *real* numbers is a rude awakening.

Table 3.1: Weekly Activity Log for a 24-hour period

Day	Activity	Start	End	Total Time (min.)	Notes	Category	Wasted Minutes
Mon	Sleep	22:00	6:00	480	My criteria are based on 7 hours of sleep. Some people require 8; this is fine.	Sleep	60
	Lounging in bed	6:00	6:15	15		Procrastination	15
	Showering & shaving	6:15	6:45	30		Morning Prep	
	Looking for clothes to wear	6:45	6:55	10		Unstructured	10
	Making breakfast	6:55	7:15	20		Meal prep	
	Eating breakfast & drinking coffee	7:15	7:30	15		Meal	
	Driving to work	7:30	8:00	30	Sitting in commute traffic	Commuting /Driving	15
	Work	8:00	12:00	240		Work	
	Lunch with co-workers	12:00	13:20	80	Hanging out with friends	Personal Time	50
	Work	13:20	17:00	220		Work	
	Driving home	17:00	17:40	40	Sitting in commute traffic	Commuting /Driving	15
	Look for gym clothes	17:40	17:45	5		Unstructured	5
	Changing for gym & grabbing snack	17:45	18:00	15		Meal	
	Driving to gym	18:00	18:10	10		Commuting /Driving	
	Socializing at the gym	18:10	18:20	10		Personal Time	5
	Exercise	18:20	19:20	60		Physical Activity	
	Driving home	19:20	19:40	20		Commuting /Driving	
	Taking shower	19:40	19:50	10		Evening Prep	
	Making dinner	19:50	20:20	30		Evening Prep	
	Eating dinner & watching TV	20:20	21:50	90		Meal	45

Day	Activity	Start	End	Total Time (min.)	Notes	Category	Wasted Minutes
	Meditation & prayer	21:50	22:00	10		Spiritual	
	Brushing teeth & get ready for bed - perhaps catch a little TV (e.g., news)	22:00	22:30	30		Evening Prep	
							Total=220
Tue	Sleep	22:30	6:00	450	Based on 7 hours of sleep	Sleep	30
	Lounging in bed	6:00	6:20	20		Procrastination	20
	Showering & shaving	6:20	6:40	20		Morning Prep	
	Looking for clothes to wear	6:40	6:50	10		Unstructured	10
	Buying breakfast (fast food)	6:50	7:20	30		Meal	
	Driving to work	7:20	8:15	55	Sitting in commute traffic	Commuting/ Driving	15
	Work	8:15	12:00	225		Work	
	Going out for lunch (fast food)	12:00	12:50	50		Personal Time	20
	Work	12:50	18:00	310		Work	
	Dropping off dry-cleaning	18:00	18:10	10		Errands	
	Driving to friend's house	18:10	18:30	20		Commuting/ Driving	
	Playing cards with friend	18:30	20:15	105		Relaxation	
	Driving home	20:15	20:30	15		Commuting/ Driving	
	Relaxing (watch TV)	20:30	21:30	60		Relaxation	60
	Surfing Internet & checking email	21:30	22:15	45	No need to surf Internet	Personal Time	25
	Meditate & pray	22:15	22:25	10		Spiritual	
	Brushing teeth & getting to bed	22:15	22:20	5		Evening Prep	
	In bed watching TV	22:20	22:45	25		Relaxation	
							Total=180

Day	Activity	Start	End	Total Time (min.)	Notes	Category	Wasted Minutes
Wed	Sleep	22:45	6:00	435	Based on 7 hours of sleep	Sleep	15
	Lounging in bed	6:00	6:30	30		Procrastination	30
	Showering & shaving	6:30	6:50	20		Morning Prep	
	Looking for clothes to wear	6:50	7:00	10		Unstructured	10
	Eating breakfast (cereal)	7:00	7:10	10		Meal	
	Checking personal email	7:10	7:20	10		Personal Time	
	Driving to work	7:20	7:55	35	Sitting in commute traffic	Commuting/ Driving	15
	Work	7:55	17:00	545		Work	
	Driving home	17:00	17:45	45	Sitting in commute traffic	Commuting/ Driving	25
	Looking for gym clothes	17:45	17:50	5		Unstructured	5
	Changing for gym & grabbing snack	17:45	18:15	30		Meal	
	Driving to the gym	18:15	18:30	15		Commuting/ Driving	
	Socializing at the gym	18:30	18:40	10		Personal Time	5
	Exercise	18:40	19:15	35		Physical Activity	
	Getting fast food	19:15	19:30	15		Personal Time	
	Driving home	19:30	19:45	15		Commuting/ Driving	
	Eating fast food	19:45	20:00	15		Meal	
	Shower & brushing teeth	20:00	20:15	15		Evening Prep	
	Checking email & surfing Internet	20:15	21:30	75	No need to surf Internet	Personal Time	45
	Meditate & pray	21:30	21:45	15		Spiritual	
	Getting ready for bed	21:45	21:50	5		Evening Prep	
	Going to bed & watch TV	21:45	22:30	45		Relaxation	
							Total=145

Day	Activity	Start	End	Total Time (min.)	Notes	Category	Wasted Minutes
Thu	Sleep	22:30	6:00	450	Based on 7 hours of sleep	Sleep	30
	Lounging in bed	6:00	6:20	20		Procrastination	20
	Showering & shaving	6:20	6:40	20		Morning Prep	
	Looking for clothes to wear	6:40	6:50	10		Unstructured	10
	Eating breakfast	6:50	7:15	25		Meal	
	Checking personal email	7:15	7:30	15		Personal Time	
	Driving to work	7:30	8:05	35	Sitting in commute traffic	Commuting/ Driving	15
	Work	8:05	15:30	445	Left early due to doctor's appointment	Work	
	Driving to doctor's office	15:30	15:45	15		Commuting/ Driving	
	Wait in doctor's office	15:45	16:30	45	Doing nothing	Waiting	45
	Time with doctor	16:30	17:10	40		Appointment	
	Driving home	17:10	17:45	35		Commuting/ Driving	
	Watching TV	17:45	18:30	45		Relaxation	45
	Eating frozen dinner	18:30	18:45	15		Meal	
	Surfing Internet & checking email	18:45	20:15	90	No need to surf Internet	Personal Time	60
	Paying bills	20:15	21:00	45		Administrative	
	Meditation & prayer	21:00	21:15	15		Spiritual	
	Brushing teeth & getting to bed	21:15	21:20	5		Evening Prep	
	Going to bed & watching TV	21:20	21:45	25		Relaxation	
							Total=225

Day	Activity	Start	End	Total Time (min.)	Notes	Category	Wasted Minutes
Fri	Sleep	21:45	6:00	495	7 hours of sleep-sufficient	Sleep	75
	Lounging in bed	6:00	6:30	30		Procrastination	30
	Showering & shaving	6:30	6:50	20		Morning Prep	
	Looking for clothes to wear	6:50	7:00	10		Unstructured	10
	Buying coffee & breakfast	7:00	7:20	20		Meal	
	Driving to work	7:20	7:55	35		Commuting/Driving	15
	Work	7:55	12:00	245		Work	
	Going out to lunch (fast food)	12:00	13:25	85	Bring your own meal	Personal Time	55
	Work	13:25	18:00	275		Work	
	Meeting friend for dinner	18:00	20:00	120		Personal Time	
	Driving home	20:00	20:20	20		Commuting/Driving	
	Playing video games	20:20	21:30	70		Personal Time	
	Checking email & surf Internet	21:30	22:45	75	Spent aimlessly surfing Internet	Personal Time	55
	Prayer & meditation	22:45	23:00	15		Spiritual	
	Brushing teeth & getting ready for bed	23:00	23:05	5		Evening Prep	
	Going to bed & watching TV	23:05	0:30	85		Relaxation	
							Total=240

Day	Activity	Start	End	Total Time (min.)	Notes	Category	Wasted Minutes
Sat	Sleep	0:30	10:00	570	Weekend (8 hrs.- sufficient)	Sleep	120
	Lounging in bed	10:00	10:30	30		Procrastination	30
	Brush teeth, wash face	10:30	10:35	5		Morning Prep	
	Eating breakfast (cereal)	10:35	10:50	15		Meal	
	Surfing Internet & checking email	10:50	12:55	125	ok-weekend relaxation	Personal Time	
	Looking for gym clothes	12:55	13:05	10		Unstructured	10
	Driving to the gym	13:05	13:20	15		Commuting/ Driving	
	Exercise	13:20	14:00	40		Physical Activity	
	Mingle with people	14:00	14:15	15		Personal Time	
	Getting some lunch (fast food)	14:15	15:00	45		Meal	
	Driving home	15:00	15:15	15		Commuting/ Driving	
	Watching a baseball game on TV	15:15	17:00	105		Relaxation	105
	Taking shower: prep to go out	17:00	17:45	45		Evening Prep	
	Meeting friend for dinner	17:45	19:30	105		Personal Time	
	Going to a movie	19:30	22:00	150		Personal Time	
	Driving home	22:00	22:15	15		Commuting/ Driving	
	Check email & surf Internet	22:15	0:30	135	No need to surf Internet again	Personal Time	115
	Prayer & meditation	0:30	0:45	15		Spiritual	
	Brushing teeth & getting ready for bed	0:45	0:50	5		Evening Prep	
	Going to bed & watching TV	0:50	2:00	70		Relaxation	
							Total=380

Day	Activity	Start	End	Total Time (min.)	Notes	Category	Wasted Minutes
Sun	Sleep	2:00	10:45	525	Weekend (8 hrs.-sufficient)	Sleep	45
	Lounge in bed	10:45	11:10	25		Procrastination	25
	Brush teeth, wash face	11:10	11:15	5		Morning Prep	
	Eating breakfast (cook eggs)	11:15	11:45	30		Meal	
	Surfing the Internet	11:45	12:30	45	ok-weekend relaxation	Personal Time	
	Watching a baseball game on TV	12:30	14:30	120		Relaxation	120
	Getting lunch	14:30	14:45	15		Commuting/ Driving	
	Eating lunch	14:45	15:00	15		Meal	
	Driving home	15:00	15:15	15		Commuting/ Driving	
	Grocery shopping	15:15	16:00	45		Errand	
	Doing laundry and cleaning apt	16:00	17:30	90		Personal Time	
	Surfing Internet & checking email	17:30	18:15	45	ok-weekend relaxation	Personal Time	
	Eating dinner	18:15	19:00	45		Meal	
	Meditation & prayer	19:00	19:15	15		Spiritual	
	Brushing teeth & getting ready for bed	19:15	19:20	5		Evening Prep	
	Going to bed & watching TV	19:20	22:00	160		Relaxation	
							Total=230

CATEGORY			AVG	Category Total (Minutes)
Sleep			486	3405
Procrastination			25	150
Morning Prep			17	120
Meal			28	415
Personal Time			66	1460

	Relaxation			77	845
	Commuting/ Driving			24	415
	Errand			45	45
	Spiritual			14	95
	Evening Prep			15	60
	Relaxation			77	845
	Unstructured			9	65
	Meal			20	20
	Physical Activity			45	135

Assess Work-Related Activities

Since your career or business utilizes an exorbitant amount of time, typically more than one third of your life, it's important to see how ineffective people can be. Below is a sample activity log from a typical salaried employee's workday. As you can see, this person wastes several hours a day not staying focused on his most critical activities. He or she is easily distracted by email, personal calls, idle chitchat, and going out to lunch frequently. Table 3.2 below is an example of an Activity Log for a typical workday.

Table 3.2: Sample Activity Log—Typical Work Day

Day	Start	End	Total Time (min.)	Notes	Category	Time Wasted
Mon	8:00	8:10	10	Get coffee and talk to colleague	Personal Time	5
	8:10	8:35	25	Email (inbox not organized)	Email	15
	8:35	8:40	5	Bathroom break	Personal Time	
	8:40	8:50	10	Look for paperwork	Administration	10
	8:40	9:00	20	Work on project	Work	
	9:00	9:10	10	Email (inbox not organized)	Email	5
	9:10	9:25	15	Work on project	Work	
	9:25	9:30	5	Personal call	Personal Time	5
	9:30	10:05	35	Meeting	Meeting	
	10:05	10:20	15	Email (inbox not organized)	Email	5

10:20	10:30	10	Chitchat with colleague	Personal Time	10
10:30	11:35	65	Work on project	Work	
11:35	11:45	10	Personal call	Personal Time	10
11:45	12:00	15	Email (inbox not organized)	Email	5
12:00	13:10	70	Out to lunch with colleague	Personal Time	40
13:10	13:20	10	Email (inbox not organized)	Email	5
13:20	13:30	10	Look for documents	Administration	10
13:30	14:00	30	Meeting	Meeting	
14:00	14:15	15	Email (inbox not organized)	Email	5
14:15	14:25	10	Get coffee	Personal Time	5
14:25	15:00	35	Work on project	Work	
15:00	16:00	60	Meeting	Meeting	
16:00	16:20	20	Email (inbox not organized)	Email	10
16:20	17:00	40	Work on project	Work	
17:00	17:10	10	Email (inbox not organized)	Work	5
				TOTAL	150 min

Employees waste a lot of time at the office—it's no surprise they struggle to complete their work on any given day. They end up trying to catch up by working nights and weekends. This often puts a strain on their relationship. It's no wonder so many marriages fail.

Document Time Wasters

Once you've documented your daily activities, let's take a look at some of the more common areas where time is used ineffectively. Review Table 3.3 below for examples of common time wasters. How much time are you wasting each day?

Table 3.3: Common Time Wasters

Category	Common Time Wasters
Career	Engaging in impromptu hallway meetings—babbling with colleagues.
	Poor meeting management: • Not having an agenda. • The meeting didn't start as advertised.
	Procrastinating—putting your projects off until the last minute.
	Going out to lunch during the week.
	Something negative that happened but was out of your control.
	Trying to do everything yourself instead of building the appropriate relationships and leveraging resources.
	Attending too many meetings.
	Email: • Interrupting your workflow by checking email frequently. • Having disorganized directories. • Not maintaining your inbox.
	Chitchatting with people who can't really help you excel in your career.
	Being in the same job function for several years.
Health	In the gym socializing instead of exercising.
	Ineffective exercise routine.
	Resting too much between exercise routines.
	Dieting instead of managing your weight.
	Not performing exercises properly.
Relationships	Getting into stupid and endless arguments that go on for hours and days sometimes. How much potentially productive time do you waste because you let those negative emotions get the best of you?
	Not communicating with your significant other effectively: • Assuming your partner can read your mind. • Making critical decisions separately which cause arguments later.
	Spending too much time with friends (e.g., in person, on the telephone, via email or texting).
	Spending time with people you don't like.
	Being a yes-person.

	Family drama.
Sleep	Sleeping too much each night.
	Lounging around in bed each morning.
Miscellaneous	Watching TV.
	Playing video games.
	Surfing the Internet.
	Constantly taking smoke breaks.
	Waiting for people. Waiting in a reception room for a doctor appointment and not being prepared by bringing reading material homework or other work.
	Daydreaming and hoping for the best to happen.
	Dwelling on the past.
	Trying to find things because you're not organized.
	Trying to figure out what to do next (each day).
	Not having your work clothes picked out the night before.
	Not being focused each day.
	Not having a daily or weekend routine.
	Consuming your resources on insignificant things instead of focusing on your priorities and daily milestones.
	Starting a project (e.g., learning a language), then abandoning it.
	Helping a friend with a project which you don't have time for.
	Doing things you don't like because you're "supposed to."
	Establishing New Year's resolutions without using proper goal management techniques.
	Sitting around while your computer is loading or booting up.
	Sitting in traffic each day.
	Not effectively managing your email inbox.
	Not focusing on one project at a time.

That's quite a list—and it's really just the tip of the iceberg. And you wonder why so many people can never accomplish their goals? Individuals waste an average of four hours a day. That's two months a year of potentially productive time subtracted from their life *every* year.

Always examine lost resources! It will be eye-opening. The purpose of this exercise is to raise your awareness of how much time can be wasted or stolen.

Extrapolate Wasted Time

Most people rate their productivity in days. For example "I was fairly productive today—I only procrastinated for a few hours throughout the day." For most, that's fine. They can live with that. Typically, they'll say "tomorrow is another day." This is a huge mistake. Change your mindset!

Don't look at lost time in minutes, hours or days. Extrapolate wasted time over a year. Visualize wasting thirty minutes a day for a year. In thirty days that's approximately fifteen hours of lost productivity; that equates to one hundred eighty hours a year squandered.

Determine Baseline Numbers

Determine your most important criteria for success. Once you determine the criteria, look at your current numbers. Examples of criteria that are important to you could be how much sleep you get every night or how much quality time you spend with family.

Establish New Baseline Numbers

Once you know your current numbers, you need to know how much time you *should be investing* to achieve your goals. Each of these actions needs to have a new baseline number associated with it. The definition of *baseline* is a measurement, calculation or location used as a basis for comparison. Document your new baseline numbers. Table 3.4 below has examples of some criteria that I believe to be important.

Table 3.4: Baseline Numbers

Category	Current Numbers (For Key Criteria)	Establish New Baseline Numbers
Sleep	Getting the proper rest is essential but not abusing sleep is even more important. People have a tendency to waste countless hours over-sleeping. How long do you currently sleep on weekdays/weekends?	**Here comes my legal disclaimer: I am not a medical doctor and I am offering my own life experiences only as information for you. Many experts believe that 7 hours of sleep is sufficient for a man or woman. Your New Baseline Number:

	Lounging around in bed for an extra 5, 10, 20 minutes or more will not help you in any way. It only adds up to many hours of wasted time. How long does it take you to get out of bed—5, 10, 20, 30, minutes?	Get out of bed immediately! If you can't—try limiting it to a maximum of 5 minutes. Your New Baseline Number:
Career	The competition is plentiful in the marketplace. You need to get management's attention. How much time do you currently spend strategizing for your career (promotion, skills development, new job, business)? How much extra time should you invest to remain on your boss's radar screen (e.g., nights and weekends)?	If you have access to email 24-7, then reply to email from management during off-business hours whenever possible. Management checks the date/time stamp on emails from their employees. Let them see that you're a company person. Also get to work before your boss and stay after they leave—whenever possible. Your New Baseline Number:
	How much time do you currently spend nurturing key relationships at work?	Identify the key players that can help you advance your career. Determine the time needed to invest nurturing these relationships. This is a must! You should devote a minimum of 2 hours a week. Your New Baseline Number:
Education	How much time do you currently spend studying?	How many hours should you spend studying in order to improve your chances of getting a 3.5 GPA or better? Your New Baseline Number:
Finances	What's the current balance in your savings account?	It's never enough. You need to beat the old number constantly—even if it's only by one dollar—it's a wonderful sense of accomplishment. Deposit some minimal amount into your savings account every time you get paid. This keeps the number fresh in your mind. Your New Baseline Number:

	How much are your bills each month?	Always look at ways to reduce your bills—reduce interest debt ASAP—reduce miscellaneous expenditures ASAP. (See Appendix B on ways to manage your finances effectively). Constantly be aware of your expenditures—try to lower that monthly number! Maintain a budget to determine an expense allowance. Your New Baseline Number:
	How much do you spend on incidentals (e.g., lunch, gourmet coffee)?	Your New Baseline Number:
	How much are you paying in interest debt?	Your New Baseline Number:
	What's your gross income for the month?	Most people need to earn extra income—how much more do you need to make to live a comfortable lifestyle? How much do you need to earn to be successful? Know that number and do something about it. Your New Baseline Number:
	What's your net income?	Your New Baseline Number:
	How much have you spent on miscellaneous finance fees (e.g., bank, credit union) over this past year?	Eliminate this ASAP—find a bank that doesn't charge erroneous fees. Your New Baseline Number: 0
Health	How many times a week are you eating junk food?	Eliminate or reduce this number. If it's more than once a week—reduce it. Your New Baseline Number:
	How many days a week are you exercising?	I believe you should do some form of exercise daily. Doing exercise daily doesn't mean going to the gym. You could wash the car one day, clean the kitchen or take a brisk walk around the block—these are all forms of exercise. Your New Baseline Number:

	How long do you spend exercising when you go to the gym or when you run?	What's the ideal number for you? Always try to beat that number—even if it's only by a few minutes—congratulations! Your New Baseline Number:
	How much alcohol do you consume?	Eliminate or reduce it. Your New Baseline Number:
	How many glasses of water do you drink each day?	You need at least 8 x 8 ounce glasses of water per day or 1.9 liters. Your New Baseline Number:
Relation-ships	How much quality time do you currently spend with family?	Maintaining a quality home life is always important! Your New Baseline Number:

What are your most critical activities? How much time are you currently spending on them? How much time should you be spending on them? This is where the rubber meets the road. You need to know and manage your numbers!

Optimize Sleep

To master time, you *must* effectively manage your sleep. Individuals waste countless hours lounging in bed, either over-sleeping or endlessly hitting the snooze button to get a few extra minutes. Then there are those ridiculous excuses: "I'm not very productive today; I didn't get my eight hours of sleep last night." I've heard this one countless times.

Techniques

If you eat properly and exercise consistently you will find out exactly how much sleep you really need for yourself. I cut my sleep down to four hours a night. *I don't recommend four hours specifically to anyone else.* In order to cut back on your sleep you *must* eat right and exercise regularly. And you should consult with a medical expert. I can't stress this point enough! Poor sleep habits may be rooted in a bad diet, eating habits, stress or medications.

There are professionals who specialize in treating this complex disorder. Figure out how much sleep your body needs to function at its optimum level. Average it out over a four-to-six-week period and stick to it until it becomes habit. Tiredness in itself is a habit that can be broken. If you've been waking up early since childhood you're probably still doing that through force of habit. You've trained your mind and your internal clock is set based on repetition. Change your mind and your internal clock will automatically change with it.

If you want to cut back on your sleep, you must take it gradually. You'll need to train your mind and body (refer to the Accountability section) in the same way you would build endurance in the gym. Just think if you had an extra hour each day to do what you want. That extra hour will allow you to accomplish so much more than you ever thought possible. The fact that you gave up your sleep for it makes it that much more sacred. I guarantee you'll make the best of that additional time. When people ask me "Wouldn't you like to sleep a few extra hours?" My response is always the same: "I will sleep plenty when I die." Now, hey, I am human. There are days when I push myself so hard it warrants a ten-to-twenty-minute power nap—if my schedule permits, of course.

When We Can't Sleep

Why do we have trouble sleeping the night before that first day of school or when starting a new job? It's the excitement and anticipation of the next day. Sometimes your mind is so full of thoughts that it simply keeps on going, totally screwing any plans of sleeping you may have had. We've all been there, watching the clock wide-eyed until about two hours before we have to go to work. I quit fighting it years ago. Here is what I do: get out of bed and get busy doing something instead of wasting those hours tossing and turning in bed. Once my mind gets focused on something else, I can return to sleep. If you have insomnia, seek medical advice.

Make It a Goal

I treat sleep as a goal, as opposed to a physical necessity. Just because people say you need a certain number of hours of sleep a night doesn't make it so. When I was in my early teens I slept eight hours a night on weekdays and ten on weekends. I was no different than any other teenager. As I was acquiring discipline, my confidence was growing along with my list of goals. I decided that excessive sleep was a waste of time because I had too many things I wanted to accomplish.

I established a goal to cut my sleep down gradually (thirty minutes at a time) until I was able to get my sleep down to four hours a night. It was a very aggressive goal and I didn't know how my body would react, so I went slowly. Every time I cut back on my sleep for thirty minutes I would give my body three to four weeks to adjust before taking on anymore. Why four hours? I really don't know, but it's worked for more than thirty years.

Train Your Mind to Sleep Less

I treat the number of hours I sleep like any other metric goal. For me, it's fun to challenge myself with numbers:
- ❏ With salary—how high can I go?
- ❏ With weightlifting—how much weight can I lift?
- ❏ With field and track events—how many seconds can I shave off my time—how low can I go?

Playing with numbers is fun. So why can't we play with the number of hours we sleep? You can and that's exactly what I've been doing for the past three decades. Train your mind to drive those numbers down to the bare minimum. If you feel rested and you're productive during the day, then you know you've got it right.

In the Accountability section, I go into further detail on how to train the mind to help you get out of bed promptly. Below are some helpful tips on how to sleep optimally.
- ❏ Get out of bed promptly.
  - Wake up with a purpose. Be passionate about something (e.g., business, career, exercise routine). Something that excites you.
  - Use multiple alarm clocks if need be. Move your alarm clock or cellular phone out of arm's reach.
  - Plan important things in the morning.
- ❏ Eat healthy and don't eat too much—especially before going to bed.
- ❏ Exercise every day. It will improve the quality of your sleep.
- ❏ Go to bed the same time each evening and wake up the same

time each day (even weekends—as close to it as possible).

❏ Don't surf the Internet or check email before going to bed.

❏ Avoid caffeine and alcohol in the evening.

❏ Sleep less. Most people oversleep. Seven hours should be sufficient for most. If you sleep more than seven hours and you would like to sleep less, then gradually cut back; however, if you do not exercise and eat healthy consistently then I wouldn't recommend it.

❏ You can still be creative and energetic on less than seven hours of sleep. If you sleep as little as I do, then you may need to take a power nap to reenergize.

❏ Don't force yourself to stay up longer to complete a work-related deadline if you're exhausted. It will be extremely difficult to be creative and the quality of work won't be as good. It's best to get to sleep early and wake up refreshed *earlier* in the morning. You will be exponentially more creative and productive.

We're Not Alone

Anyone who has been through military basic training can confirm the effectiveness of minimum sleep coupled with physical conditioning. Sometimes its two to three hours a night for up to six weeks. Not only do recruits survive the experience, they are forced to realize what they are capable of accomplishing. It's only temporary for them, but it's a full-time job for their drill instructors. Have you ever seen a Marine drill instructor (DI)? They all look like any Marine ad or poster you've ever seen. The DIs and their recruits running in cadence behind them are alert and in the best shape of their life. Being kept on a strict regimen of minimum sleep has enhanced their lives forever.

Statistics show that about twenty percent of Americans are employed in some kind of shift work. There are too many to list here, but some that come to mind are the transportation industry, the food industry and the military. Some do work that requires an extremely high degree of concentration. Submariners and air traffic controllers are a couple of them.

The Naval Submarine Medical Research Laboratory performs watch-standing studies. They have experimented with all kinds of alternative watch and sleep schedules to increase operational performance as well as better the quality of life for submariners. They have examined what is best to suit their function. Everyone should toy with this concept to streamline sleep schedules for themselves. Whether you're a genuine Navy submariner or an avid submarine sandwich eater you can do this.

Extensive research has also been done on air traffic controllers. Research on thirty-seven air traffic controllers in Jacksonville found that those with frequent shift changes, including the after-midnight graveyard shift, were better able to focus on the tasks at hand during the day. Raymon McAdaragh did the study for his doctorate at The University of Florida at Jacksonville in instruction and curriculum. "What I learned is the opposite of what you would expect. People on rapidly rotating schedules that include graveyard shift have better attention allocation, quicker reaction times and are better able to learn cognitive tasks during the day shift."

The point is, there are variables not being utilized because no one bothered to do the research. We can learn from others who already realize that sleep is an adjustable option that is well worth further exploration.

Make Every Minute Count

"Time is the scarcest resource and unless it is managed, nothing else can be managed."
Peter F. Drucker

Peter Drucker hit the nail right on the head. How many people do you know of that manage their life down to the minute? I bet none. Did you ever stop to think why people always run out of time at the end of the day? Rarely do they get everything done for any given day. These days' time *must* be managed in order to accomplish as much as possible in twenty-four hours.

Eliminate Unnecessary Drama

We all know people who could be considered toxic. These toxic people can absorb enormous amounts of your time and drain your life energy. Do you have a friend who is always dumping on you? You listen to hours of gossip about the latest boyfriend? What is the exchange in that? She keeps repeating the same pattern. You've wasted not only the time she spent talking to you about it, but also the time you spent worrying about it.

Emotional vampires know that if they can get you to feel sorry for them that they have won. Your emotional energy and time gets drained and they get fed. Do you really want to continue this unhealthy behavior? Make excuses (tell little white lies). Stop wasting your precious resources.

Don't Sit Around Wasting Time

"The great French Marshall Lyautey once asked his gardener to plant a tree. The gardener objected that the tree was slow-growing and would not reach maturity for 100 years. The Marshall replied, "In that case, there is no time to lose; plant it this afternoon!"
John F. Kennedy

Every minute counts, especially when you're trying to get ahead of the game and accomplish so much in life. There are many instances where we can look back and see where we threw away valuable minutes which added up to hours, days or even months. That wasted time could have been used to turn some of your dreams into reality. Twenty or thirty years ago, there wasn't as much pressure to do so much in such little time. We had the luxury of sitting around doing nothing whenever we had the opportunity:

- ❏ When you sat around in the doctor's office for your appointment—it didn't matter how long you waited, you just picked up a magazine and started reading.
- ❏ When you got a haircut, sometimes you had to wait if your stylist was running a bit late. Again, it was no big deal: you read a magazine.
- ❏ When you took your car to the mechanic, you could wait for a few hours. No big deal.

In most instances there was a lack of urgency on your part. Times have changed. Perhaps it's because of the incredible pace of technology, corporate competition, or the economy. Whatever the reason, the era of doing more with less is here to stay.

Can you really afford to sit around and do nothing? I don't think so. Always be prepared. Bring along some of your work—whatever that may be. I bring my laptop computer or a hard copy printout of the latest manuscript whenever I go to appointments. If there isn't a long wait—so be it, then I haven't wasted my time. But at least I'm prepared if they're behind schedule. Even if you don't own a laptop, bring along a book you've wanted to read. You can even start writing a book, do your school work, or just bring along a pad of paper to take some notes of tasks you need to get done or think of more creative ways to complete your goals ahead of schedule.

"What is a thousand years? Time is short for one who thinks, endless for one who yearns."
Alain

Equate Time with Money

Why in the world would anyone equate time with money? A very simple answer: more than one third of your lifetime is spent working. Your employer pays you a salary based on your skills, experience, hard work, and dedication. One-third for most of you is spent sleeping. The remainder is what you make of it. It's your time, but unfortunately, time is limited and sooner or later you will die—that's a guarantee.

"Lost wealth may be replaced by industry, lost knowledge by study, lost health by temperature or medicine, but lost time is gone forever."
Samuel Smiles

Life is too short: why not get the most out of it? I equate time with money because time is precious and scarce. Most people don't like to throw money away because it takes too much time and effort to earn it. In our society, you won't get very far without money. So, if our time is scarce and precious the only logical thing to do is equate every minute with some monetary value. Every minute should have a price tag associated with it. Not every hour, but every *minute*. I promise you that your time could not be better spent than reading what follows.

By far the No. 1 excuse people share with me is that they don't have enough time on any given day. I beg to differ, because the tables you filled out in this section paint a totally different picture. They highlight how much time people waste on any given day.

Associating a price for a day or a month won't cut it. Do it for every minute of your existence. How much time can you afford to throw away?

> "You may delay, but time will not."
> *Benjamin Franklin*

How much is a minute worth to you? Being self-employed, I set my price at $10.00 a minute. Why ten? I wanted a hefty price tag associated with each day (a day equates to 1440 minutes). If you're an employee, take your yearly salary and divided it by the number of minutes you work a day.

Imagine that there is a bank that credits your account each morning with $86,400. It carries over no balance from day to day. Every evening deletes whatever part of the balance you failed to use during the day. What would you do? Draw out ALL OF IT, of course!

Each of us has such a bank. Its name is TIME. Every morning, it credits you with 86,400 seconds. Every night it writes off, as lost, whatever of this you have failed to invest to good purpose. It carries over no balance. It allows no overdraft. Each day it opens a new account for you. Each night it burns the remains of the day. If you fail to use the day's deposits, the loss is yours.

There is no going back. There is no drawing against what future days will or will not bring. You must live in the present on today's deposits and invest wisely so as to get from it the utmost in health, happiness, and success! The clock is running. Make the most of today. Table 3.5 below highlights a few tips on effective time management practices.

Table 3.5: Effective Time Management Practices

Ineffective Time Management	Effective Time Management
Sitting around and doing nothing except staring at four walls. Perhaps you're at a barber shop and there are three people waiting before you to get a haircut. Or you're in the waiting room and the doctor is running way behind schedule.	When are doctors, dentists or even your barber ever on schedule? Bring reading material, bring writing material—don't just sit there doing nothing.
You're stuck in a long boring meeting with a room full of people—the meeting agenda has nothing to do with you but your boss wanted you there.	Look attentive, but focus on your own agenda: • Bring a notepad or bring in one of your work assignments (perhaps something that you can print out)—make sure you sit in the back of the room or close to it. • You can also bring in your laptop and work on your projects—make sure you look at the speaker occasionally so it looks like you're taking notes from the meeting.
You're waiting for your slow computer to boot up or reboot.	Organize your work area. Update your to-do list.
Waiting at the airport for your flight or sitting on the airplane doing nothing.	Work on your laptop. If you don't have a laptop—catch up on email via your mobile device. If you don't have one, bring along a notepad and strategize how to improve your life or perhaps start a daily journal to track progress.
You're in the kitchen waiting for your roast to finish baking.	Clean up the area: maybe wash dishes, sweep the floor—do something—don't just sit there staring at the oven.
You work out of your home office—you've been working for nine straight hours and you're starting to get tired, your productivity has slowed down considerably—however it's too early to go to sleep—it's not even dark outside…	Don't try and push it. Get up and do something else. Once you get up and do something else, you will recharge your batteries and can come back and do some work that's not brain-intensive. • Spend twenty to thirty minutes cleaning your bedroom or the garage. • Organize your office. • Clean up some old files on your computer. • Organize your files.
Crawling along in commute traffic when you have alternative options.	Get up earlier and avoid the traffic. • Get to work earlier if management allows it and you don't have any family obligations in the morning. • Or go to a gym close to work or close to home—work out first (avoiding traffic), then get to work.

Lying in bed an extra five, ten, or twenty minutes in the morning.	Jump out of bed when it's time to get up—an extra few minutes of sleep doesn't buy you anything except more wasted minutes.
Waiting for your significant other for a long period of time.	My wife had surgery last year—I drove her to therapy three times a week. I waited in the car for one hour each visit. I brought my laptop and actually finished off a good portion of this material in the car waiting.

Some of the examples only save a few minutes—but that's the point: throughout the day and evening there are many things that you can do differently to save valuable minutes which add up to hours, days, weeks and months of precious time.

Manage Energy for Peak Performance

Some people are more productive in the evening; others are more productive in the morning. Whichever works best, perform brain-intensive activities during your productive hours and do less brain-intensive activities such as administrative functions when you are not at your peak. Table 3.6 below is an example of an Activity Log of someone who is very efficient and is not wasting any time (in a twenty-four-hour period).

Table 3.6: Daily Activity Log for Someone Who is Efficient

Day	Activity	Start	End	Total Time (min.)	Notes	Category
Mon	Sleep	21:30	4:30	420		Sleep
	Eat a snack & brush teeth	4:30	4:40	10		Morning Prep
	Drive to gym	4:40	4:50	10		Commuting/ Driving
	Exercise	4:50	5:45	55		Physical Activity
	Drive home	5:45	5:55	10		Meal Prep
	Eat breakfast & shower	5:55	6:30	35		Meal
	Drive to work	6:30	6:45	15		Commuting/ Driving
	Work	6:45	15:00	495	Eat lunch while working	Work
	Drive home	15:00	15:15	15	Beat the traffic	Commuting/ Driving
	Cook dinner & eat	15:15	16:00	45	TV on news station	Meal
	Work on email & work project	16:00	17:45	105		Work
	Write to-do list	17:45	17:50	5		Administrative
	Clean up dishes & clothes	17:50	18:05	15		Clean up
	Pull clothes for next day	18:05	18:10	5		Evening Prep
	Read a book	18:10	20:00	110		Personal Development
	Meditate & pray	20:00	20:40	40		Spiritual
	Brush teeth, floss & get ready for bed	20:40	20:50	10		Evening Prep
	Speak with girlfriend	20:50	21:10	20		Relationship Management
	Go to bed & watch TV	21:10	21:30	20		Relaxation

Dos and Don'ts of Successful Time Management

Managing time effectively means changing the way you operate. How would I do things differently? Some of this material may be a repeat of content I've discussed throughout this section but I thought it would be important to summarize the key points in one area.

- ❏ Sleep only seven hours (or less).
- ❏ Get out of bed immediately.
- ❏ Exercise in the morning.
- ❏ Try to avoid commute traffic. If you have no family obligations—leave the house up to a few hours earlier—even if you get to your destination an hour earlier, go to a coffee shop and work on your laptop.
- ❏ Don't go out to lunch with your buddies a few times a week (once a week is sufficient).
- ❏ Maintain structure. Lay out your clothes the night before, remain organized and follow a to-do list every day.
- ❏ Don't surf the Internet aimlessly—read a book or organize your files.
- ❏ Only watch TV when you're cooking or eating dinner for relaxation.

Summary

Most people waste several hours every day, but that doesn't seem to faze them. It's the same old response: "Tomorrow is another day." If things are too comfortable for us, we tend to coast along, forgetting that time is passing, oblivious to the fact that we are not accomplishing our goals. We get distracted easily. Oh, and how we make plenty of excuses.

Some of the best excuses have to do with *tomorrow* or *later*. Your mind will say things like "I have plenty of time to complete my goals—I'm only twenty years old," or "I still have 3 months to complete my goal—what's the rush?" The trouble is that tomorrow comes and the goal has not been achieved.

In this section (Step 3) I educated you on how to *permanently* change your mentality about time. To change a mindset that's been engraved in our society for eons is no easy task—but it is doable. Managing time efficiently is managing your life like a business—a successful business! When you own a business you know every aspect of the operations (every number). To become profitable you need to know and manage your numbers—sales, customer base, expenses, revenue per employee. Now get serious about your life and manage your numbers to be successful.

❏ How much time is actually used for each of your activities?

❏ How much time do you actually waste? Understand time wasters and how to categorize your activities to see where the bulk of your time is being utilized.

❏ How much time should you be spending on your activities?

❏ Evaluate your work-related activities in detail. Work consumes half of many people's lives, especially if you include time-suckers like commute time, evening emails and phone calls and catching up on projects over the weekend. The objective for evaluating your professional life in detail is to see where you waste resources, which will allow you to make the necessary changes to become more efficient throughout your workday. You will eventually have more of a balanced lifestyle away from the office.

❏ Extrapolate time wasted (per activity) throughout the year. It's eye-opening. If you are like most people, you waste approximately three months a year. That's a quarter of your life.

❏ Identify your most important activities. Which ones are most critical for success? How much time are you currently spending in these areas? How much time should you be spending in these areas to achieve success? I refer to this time as your baseline numbers.

Once you have a handle on your numbers then equate time (minutes not hours) with money. Put a price on your time—how much is it worth?

You have one lifetime to play the game you're currently engaged in. So the moral of this section (Step 3) is to treat time as the precious resource it is and utilize it fully.

STEP 4: HOLD YOURSELF ACCOUNTABLE

What Is Accountability?

In the first three sections Steps 1-3, I provided you with the knowledge on how to *institute structure, prioritize your life* and *master time.* The most difficult aspect of personal and professional growth is holding yourself accountable every day. Most individuals can hold themselves accountable for a few weeks because they've just read the latest and greatest self-help book, listened to a motivational CD, are still excited about the new year and their freshly heralded resolution, or have attended a seminar on success. Short-term fixes only work for a few days or weeks and then it's back to an unproductive lifestyle —no motivation and no accountability.

Accountability means taking responsibility for your actions and keeping your commitments. Our society is successful because we hold ourselves accountable to our jobs—mostly out of necessity. After all, we have to eat and pay our bills. Unfortunately, for most people, accountability stops there. Our mind tells us: *Hey, it's five PM, time to quit work for the day.*

To be successful means being productive and around the clock. It's being your own boss—and being accountable to yourself when you leave the office.

Trust and Confidence

Holding yourself accountable every day builds trust and earns the confidence of others. When you trust yourself to always deliver. This builds confidence, and therefore people are drawn to you and want to be in a business relationship with you. They have a high regard for you because of your integrity and your unwavering determination.

The Foundation of Leadership

When individuals consistently hold themselves accountable, they are looked upon as leaders. Accountability is one of the key characteristics of a leader. Nothing breeds loyalty more than accountability. When people see that you care and you consistently keep your word, they will be loyal, productive and will follow your direction. You will build solid friendships and business relationships, which as a leader is crucial for your success. Below is a process flow defining accountability.

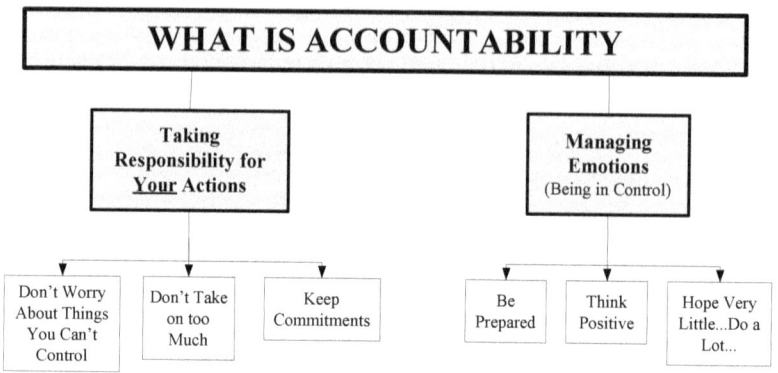

There is No Such Thing as "We"

I'm convinced that some people could not exist very long without an endless stream of assistance. Those they depend on are enablers and the best thing they could do is to break your cycle of dependence on them, otherwise it will never end. What becomes of them when they lose those they rely on so heavily? There's nothing wrong with having a support network for stressful times. The problem is that dependent people live their lives driving one-way down the *stress lane* because of their total reliance on others. They create their own stress by having to manage so many other people who are doing their work for them. I'm referring to constant dependence due to sheer laziness and lack of discipline.

You shouldn't depend on others as a rule. You need to count on yourself to make things happen. Individuals who rely on others for help seem to end up being disappointed more often than not. Do you honestly think your friends and colleagues will pay your bills? Maybe they will and maybe they won't—do you really like those odds? Do you think you'll be able to sleep well at night?

Don't Worry About Things You Can't Control

Why bother? You waste precious cycles when there's nothing you can do about a situation. You may want to complain about your boss or a car accident that wasn't your fault, but you can't quit your job until you find something else and you can't stop driving.

Worrying about these negative situations only wastes valuable energy and time. The more cycles you take away from holding yourself accountable, the more likely you will fail to achieve your goals.

Worrying about negative things that are out of your control can cause stress-related health issues such as high blood pressure and sleeping disorders.

Learning to cope with only things or events in your control will keep you in a positive frame of mind. The objective is to focus on the things that are in your control such as your family, priorities, goals and milestones.

By accepting that you can't change everything you will have the strength and conviction to focus on the things that you can change. You can't always control what happens but you can control how you respond to the situation. You will remove the negative thoughts and move forward with conviction.

Don't Take on Too Much

Be prudent about how much you take on—don't be a yes-person. Be selective about how many commitments you make. You probably already have a full plate. Make sure you take on your obligations associated with your priorities first. If you have ample time at the end of the day and you're not that tired, then perhaps you can take on a few more tasks. However, in this fast-paced era we live in I seriously doubt that you can take on more without failing. Pick and choose your commitments carefully.

Be realistic with your goal due dates—if you establish unrealistic completion dates, you are making it much more difficult to hold yourself accountable and to succeed. If you fail to fulfill one of your obligations it is just as important to own up and make things right. It starts by admitting that you made a mistake and taking the appropriate action so it doesn't happen again. If you make a mistake, turn it into a learning experience.

Keeping Commitments

Commitment is the key to success with all endeavors. It cannot be half-hearted. It needs to be all-out, do or die. The definition of commitment is *dedication to a long-term course of action, engagement, and involvement.* The key words are *dedication* and *long-term.* Once you commit to something, you have to follow through. Each one of your goals needs full commitment in order to be successful.

> "Until one is committed, there is hesitancy, the chance to draw back, always ineffectiveness. Concerning all acts of initiative (and creation), there is one elementary truth, the ignorance of which kills countless ideas and splendid plans: that the moment one definitely commits oneself, the Providence moves too. All sorts of things occur to help one that would never otherwise have occurred. A whole stream of events issues from the decision, raising in one's favor all manner of unforeseen incidents and meetings and material assistance, which no man could have dreamt would have come his way."
> W.H. Murray

Managing Emotions

A big part of holding yourself accountable is *being in control* and maintaining an even-keel demeanor. The most important emotional skill is to face what is in front of you without letting your emotions get in the way. How do you learn to do this? Stay focused on the present and face what is being said and what is being done.

Facing things has to do with courage. Running away from conflict and unpleasant emotions means that you have relinquished power and control. Below are some general tips on dealing with emotional reactions outside of work.

- ❏ Meditate
- ❏ Role-play
- ❏ Keep a journal
- ❏ Play games in which you imagine yourself in difficult situations and imagine how you would handle them
- ❏ Keep a log so you can learn your triggers, your weak spots
- ❏ Go for a walk and notice things around you
- ❏ Really focus on the details of your environment
- ❏ Use techniques that diffuse your emotional reactions such as Emofree (an easy to use de-stressing technique—www.emofree.com)
- ❏ Draw out a situation that would be rough for you and think of many different ways to handle it—goofy, silly, mean or super

nice. The idea is to have several options for difficult situations.
❏ Expect that life will present you with challenges
❏ Become aware of your breathing, your feet, your hands

Emotions are one of life's paradoxes. Emotions tell you things; they give you feedback. They tell you what you're afraid of, when somebody is violating a boundary, what makes you happy, what you are about. Fear, anger, grief and hopelessness have their place. It's getting stuck in them that causes problems.

Being Prepared

Controlling your emotions means being prepared and planning for worst-case scenarios—emergencies happen when you least expect them. The more practice you get controlling your emotions the easier it will be to cope with unexpected:
❏ Medical emergencies
❏ Loss of employment
❏ Breakups
❏ Deaths in the family
❏ Unexpected expenses

Controlling emotions is crucial to remaining productive. It means being prepared, emotionally, to calmly and intelligently cope with disappointment or failure. How you deal with failure says more about character than dealing with success. Whether your demeanor is positive or negative below are examples of how to manage your emotions.

Example of uncontrolled emotions:

Let's say you just got a promotion. You decide to celebrate by having a few drinks after work. You party up a storm—you feel like you're on top of the world—and then you get into your car and drive. You get pulled over and get a DUI ticket and spend the night in jail. Or worse, you accidentally hurt someone. So much for your bright future.

Example of controlled emotions:

Celebrate responsibly. Have a few drinks after work and take a taxi or get a ride from a friend, or perhaps go out to dinner and celebrate with your significant other and let him or her drive.

Uncontrolled emotions can be disastrous. Do NOT be foolish and work hard to be successful for years and possibly throw it all away in one night of stupidity.

Thinking Positive

There's an old saying: *If you're always positive, good things will happen.* Unfortunately, that's not always true. Sure you *should* think positive every day of the year, but that's not realistic over the long-haul. Good things *and* bad things will happen regardless of your disposition. People may misconstrue this type of behavior as being negative, but you don't have to act negative to cope with it. Keep perspective. Know that whatever happened is a setback and learn from it. Don't drag others down with complaints and worry. They will lose confidence in you. Remain in control at all times.

Some individuals have a tendency to think positive and stop there. They won't put in the *extra* effort to *make* something positive happen on their own despite their mood. The worst *will* come, unfortunately, but when it does you're better prepared to fight through it and focus on your priorities.

Hope Very Little and Do a Lot

If you want a better life, better career or better body, stop hoping for a miracle and start making it happen on your own. Hoping for success is like playing the lottery to get rich. There is a statistical possibility it could happen—but it's unlikely The more time you spend hoping, the less effort is put into strategizing, planning and executing to improve your life.

❏ How can I accomplish my goals faster?
❏ Is there an alternative path to take in my career?
❏ How can I make better use of my time when I am at home?

People are always telling me that hoping and dreaming is good for you. I say it's overrated. Hoping and dreaming doesn't pay the bills or accomplish your goals.

Summary

Accountability is where the rubber meets the road. It's ensuring that you complete your milestones *every* day regardless of setbacks or obstacles. Even if you have an emotionally challenging day, being accountable means overcoming difficult situations. It means redirecting negative emotions into a powerful force of positive energy. It's important to get on with your life, adhering to your priorities and focusing on your milestones, not to sulk with depression. It's also being responsible for your actions and keeping your commitments every day, without failure.

Holding yourself accountable around the clock is *extremely* difficult. This is where most people falter both personally and professionally. You may do okay for a few days or weeks, but then it's back to business as usual. The urge to revert back to your unproductive, undisciplined ways is relentless.

To hold yourself accountable means being your own cop. You must enforce the actions needed to achieve your milestones. If for some reason you fail, take responsibility; never blame someone else. Implement a solution or adjust so you don't fail again. It's impossible to police yourself on a part-time basis. The only way to be responsible for your actions every day of the year is to *train your mind* to be that cop. In the next section, I educate you on how to *attain accountability* by *training your mind* to be that enforcer.

How to Attain Accountability

Holding yourself accountable begins with a shift in mentality. You need to look at your life differently. Be serious about it—formalize your self-development. Pretend you have no choice but to work a sixteen-hour shift every day and act as though you are your own boss. Hold yourself accountable because your livelihood depends on it. The work performed is on you. You're the company. In this section I educate you on how to *train your mind* to become your own boss and cop. Below is a process flow on how to attain accountability.

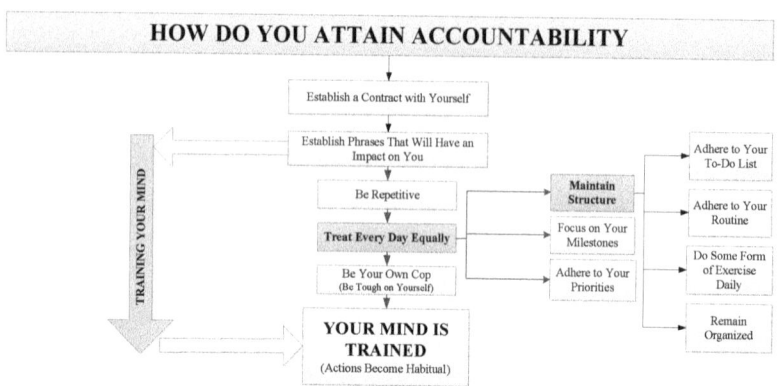

Establish a Contract with Yourself

The path towards holding yourself accountable starts with a personal contract. This contract is not a paper document; it is a paradigm shift, a culture adjustment. However, like any contract, it has rules and guidelines that you must adhere to. It is a completely new outlook on life. It runs through you constantly, like the blood that flows through your veins. It is part of your daily routine.

This contract will alter your personality. Everyone will notice it. They will see the confidence in your face and the focus in your eyes. You will feel like you can accomplish anything and everything—and you will. There will be no limitations.

It is a mental toughness; it is like having a professional trainer pushing you all day.

The Contract is Always There

My line of work involves frequent travel and interacting with people all over the world. Many wonder how anyone could travel 75 percent of the time and stay in shape. Finding the time for consistent exercise is one of the most difficult challenges in life. It's hard to maintain a daily exercise routine even when you are not always on the go. Now imagine traveling often, with different time zones playing havoc with your internal body clock, endless customer dinners and parties, lousy hotels, long flights and airport delays. On top of all that, finding a health club to exercise is a real experience, especially in certain countries.

Day in and day out, I would get up and exercise in the morning, no matter where I was, no matter what I did the night before, and regardless of what time I went to sleep. Sometimes I would work out after only two or three hours of sleep.

It is that contract with myself to exercise daily. It never goes away; it never allows me to become complacent. It has taken over my life. Even if I was exhausted, the contract subconsciously motivates me and reminds me to keep pushing. It's silly but effective. I do not own or control this contract—it controls me. My mind is trained to exercise every day. If I wanted to sleep in one morning, I would try and fight it, but most of the time, to no avail. But in the end as tired as I may have been, after I exercised, I felt great.

When I was in Bangkok, I had to speak in front of a very large audience at nine on a Thursday morning. I flew in from San Francisco, arriving at eleven Wednesday evening. When I arrived at the hotel room around midnight, I could not sleep, so I decided to go out on the town. By the time I returned it was three. The time difference between San Francisco and Bangkok is fourteen hours. The health club opened at six in the morning, and I was there for my workout. As you can imagine, I was tired, but I managed to push myself through it all.

I survived the ordeal and actually felt pretty good during my talk period. About a month later, I received pictures that were taken at the event. My face looked like I had not slept for a week.

One could argue that this is overdoing it and making myself sick. Yet, I have been *overdoing* it for over four decades—always pushing my body to the max. I was in my thirties, already very disciplined, and felt like nothing could stop me. I was beaming with confidence. I felt invincible.

The contract:

❏ Remain structured at all times
❏ Focus on your priorities
❏ Make *every* minute count
❏ Be your own cop (hold yourself accountable)
❏ Maintain personal and professional values at all times

A personal contract forces you to take a commitment seriously and stick with it. It's a betrayal to do otherwise. It helps instill the discipline needed to stay on track; it keeps you focused on long-term benefits and goals, not short-term inconvenience.

Train Your Mind

Training your mind is best described as a series of premeditated steps that you take to evoke a desired behavior. Whereas you train a muscle to perform a desired movement or motion, you train the mind to obtain desired concentration and attitude, as well as to defeat laziness.

Without such training, however, it is impossible to keep up with the growing demands of day-to-day life and goal attainment for very long, because commitments will slip through the cracks, or you will simply lack the energy to follow through and risk burnout, loss of focus, and disappointment.

Training the mind also means understanding yourself and your limits. When you know yourself, you know what you can and cannot do; you know where your boundary is drawn and you can aggressively keep extending that boundary. Without such knowledge, you are shooting in the dark and greatly risking over-commitment.

The only way to consistently push yourself is to train your mind to push your body for you. Once your mind is trained it will be that guiding force behind all your actions then, and *only* then, will you become successful. It will constantly nudge you forward even when you're tired and feeling lazy. If you attempt to move forward without properly training your mind then you will surely fail.

The Five Rs

Doctors and scientists now firmly believe that 75 percent of sickness and disease starts in the mind. Researchers have also proven that stress, which starts in the mind, is the number one cause of fatigue and illness. Imagine what would happen if we managed our minds' health. We would live healthier and more productive lives.

"Anything the mind can conceive and believe; it can achieve."
Charles Allen

In order to prepare your mind for the journey, it is important to understand the destination. Only when you have a clear picture of the desired result—the goals—can you begin to map out a plan to get there.

For instance, if your goal is to be a CEO of a major corporation one day, then the first step is to make *career* a priority in your life. The next step is to establish goals to help you achieve that objective. The point here is for you to see the *progression of thinking.* You must go, in your mind, from where you are today (an employee) to where you want to be (CEO). Not only that, but you must find the simplest, most realistic, no-nonsense way of accomplishing that task. In a linear progression, it would look something like this:

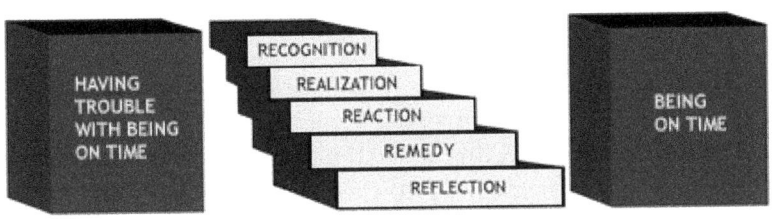

Great, so what does all of that mean? Really, it's fairly simple.

Recognition

Obviously, you must first recognize the problem or identify the trait you wish to develop. Simply by looking at your current life and routine, you should be able to quickly identify areas you would like to improve. Indeed, most of us have a lot of these, so you shouldn't be discouraged. Pinpoint exactly what you intend to improve and write a list of those traits.

By putting your thoughts in writing, you're creating a material account of your thinking and action. This will help you to accurately sort and process your thoughts and prevent anything from slipping through the cracks. In this stage of your journey, you want to be particularly thorough to avoid re-work. When you are just starting the journey towards goal attainment, thoughts and ideas will appear randomly and without order or priority. Often, it is important to capture them and organize them neatly in order to see the greater picture. Once the greater picture and the steps necessary to get there become clear, you won't need those notes. But always use them as a constructive tool to stimulate thinking and creativity as much as possible.

Realization

The next step in the progression is for you to realize what needs to be done to address the problem, behavior, or situation. This is essentially the stage where you plan the solution. Make sure you take time to think carefully about what you can change. Typically, only one or two things need to be done or approached differently in order to deal with a problem effectively.

Reaction

This is the plan-implementation step. You are now *acting upon* your decision by being responsible and taking control. This step is particularly difficult for some, because it requires stepping up to the challenge. If you can do it, however, it is the official halfway point of accomplishing your goal.

Practically speaking, this is also the place where formal training of the mind really begins. Up to this point, planning and mind-mapping have all been preparation steps, but once you begin *reacting*, that is where the real changes are going to be made.

How does one react?

The obvious question here is simple: "How do I do it?" The process is not complicated, and need not require any special knowledge or training. Really, all it will take is a set of strategically placed actions in your schedule to trigger the desired outcome and focus.

At this point, be aware of all the things you *could* and *should* be doing to improve the situation. Doing this is not difficult. In fact, it is a great opportunity to apply a little bit of discipline and get a feel for what it really means pushing yourself mentally *every* day. This is done effectively through the use of simple, straightforward, quick reminders.

At first, the task of constantly reminding yourself will seem a bit tedious. Do not let this stop you. It is merely a temporary state of discomfort that comes with modifying behavior. Discomfort creates motion; it forces a reaction. The following are steps to effectively condition the mind to be a built-in, automatic reminder of goals and priorities:

Remind yourself of your priorities

Jot down notes, write key reminder words on the bathroom mirror, leave quick text messages on your cell phone or simply program a wristwatch alarm to go off at a predetermined time during the day. This will constantly keep bringing attention back to your priorities, even though it will at first be annoying.

Repeat, repeat, and repeat

After a period of constant reminders, a funny thing will begin to happen. You will begin to anticipate the reminder. Suddenly, you'll wake up a few minutes before your alarm clock, before you walk into your bathroom, or something of the sort. When this happens, you should acknowledge it and celebrate it! This is a good sign.

Remedy

This is perhaps the most empowering state that you can experience on the way to your overall objective. It is the point where you begin seeing concrete results as a by-product of your actions. You will suddenly realize that you are getting a feel for what it was that you set out to do in the first place. It is a wonderful feeling and can be used as motivation for many challenges to come.

WARNING

Although this stage is extremely fulfilling, it can also serve as a great distraction on the path to accomplishing goals. Early taste of success can often cause a feeling of euphoria. Be careful here, and don't let the first few gulps of fresh air intoxicate you. This is a natural tendency, especially for beginners who experience success and control for the first time. Enjoy it, celebrate it, but know that this is only the beginning.

Reflection

Reflecting is an important component of the cycle, and sadly, the step that is neglected the most. Reflection is the process of looking back on progress and identifying patterns about yourself and your natural tendencies. By learning from experiences and mistakes, you can avoid making those mistakes again.

Imagine never making the same mistake twice. Some would say that this is impossible, but that's nonsense. All it takes is developing one's analytical abilities and soberly evaluating past mistakes and failures. If you take time to reflect, fantastic things will happen. You will begin to think bigger and faster. You will make decisions more accurately and quickly. You will be able to handle more challenges as times goes on. You will be calmer, relaxed, and in control.

When the train comes—hop on it

At some point, all the training will just click into place. I don't know how it happens, but it does. Perhaps a few months down the line (if you are motivated), you will suddenly realize that you no longer need the alarms, notes, or those surrounding situations. Your mind will become filled with that static charge of commitment, and it will absolutely cease to give you any rest from accomplishing goals and living by priorities. Essentially, you will no longer have to consciously think about what needs to be done.

Training the mind is not unlike playing scales on a musical instrument or performing martial arts. One must play and repeat those dozens and dozens of times before the internal mechanism picks up on the sound and rhythm. Once that happens, one will no longer need to play scales. An internal metronome will keep pace, no matter where one is or what is happening. Similarly, you must continually condition your mind until the steps towards goal achievement occur as naturally as breathing.

Training the mind doesn't have to be tedious or boring. You can make it fun by rewarding yourself along the way and, most importantly, doing it for the right reasons—*your* reasons. If you commit yourself to training your mind for a time, then you will find that your prosperity and quality of life will skyrocket in just a few short months.

Establish Phrases

When a drill sergeant barks out orders at a recruit, the recruit listens and executes ASAP. The sergeant's voice is loud and whatever phrase is used hits the mark immediately—nothing is sugarcoated. For me, certain phrases may get my attention faster than others, things like *you're lazy, you're a loser, you're a failure, do you want to be a fat slob for the rest of your life and die early?* These phrases resonate with me; which phrases will hit your hot button? Which ones will wake you up, perhaps get you upset and cause you to finally do something to improve your personal and professional life once and for all?

Some challenges in your life will require a more positive and subtle approach. Positive phrases affirm what you want. They actually condition your mind. What do you want to become or what do you want to do? I used both positive and negative phrases to train my mind. Below are examples of some of the phrases that may work for you. I've also included a few stories and helpful tips to help train your mind.

Phrases to Help You Consistently Exercise (Combat Laziness)

- ❏ Each day I exercise, the healthier I feel and the more energetic I become.
- ❏ I look pathetic—I wear clothes that hide my fat—even in the dead of summer—how long do I want to keep doing this?
- ❏ I look like shit.
- ❏ If I take today off, I'll want to take tomorrow off—this cycle will NEVER stop-JUST GO DO IT.
- ❏ I know it's hard to exercise, but just imagine what fun it will be to show off in a size six dress at my reunion. (Visualize yourself in that dress, and how you'll feel when you're getting those looks of admiration.)
- ❏ If I don't exercise today I'll look like millions of out-of-shape people (Visualize yourself and other overweight people).
- ❏ I don't want to be ashamed of my body and scared of putting on a bathing suit, do I? I want to be proud of my body.
- ❏ I'm going to die sooner than later because I am becoming obese.
- ❏ I'm a wuss—do I want to be one for the rest of my life?
- ❏ You're a lazy fat slob.
- ❏ Push yourself—you loser!
- ❏ Every day I take a break is another day wasted.
- ❏ How many days of being unproductive do I want to flush down the toilet?

Tips to Combat Laziness

It's easy to get bored with your exercise routine and lose motivation. It's easy to no longer be motivated. The first solution you think of that rears its ugly head is: "I need a break." Wrong. Below are some tips you may consider using to remain consistent. Never assume that a *break* will solve the problem. I recommend making some wholesale changes in your routine.

- ❏ I've been working out twice a week for a few months—I'll increase it to three times per week.
- ❏ I exercise for twenty minutes every day—there's no reason

why I can't increase it to twenty-five minutes now.

❏ I've been burning a minimum of four hundred calories on the treadmill consistently for weeks now. I am going to raise the bar and make the new minimum number four hundred twenty-five.

❏ I bench pressed one hundred fifty-five pounds this week for the first time. My next goal will be to press one hundred sixty pounds in the next thirty days.

❏ My weight training routine consisted of one set per exercise this entire month—next month I'm going to increase it to two sets per exercise.

❏ Tomorrow I will just do some sort of cardiovascular workout and an abdominal workout—no weight training.

❏ Next week I'm going to change my leg workout drastically. In between each exercise, I will do two minutes of cardiovascular exercise.

❏ Make your exercise routine more interesting, challenging and fun by trying to beat your previous best.

Instilling a Sense of Urgency

Over four decades ago when I was a teenager, I actually convinced myself that my life would end at the age of forty. I know this may sound morbid, but I wanted to give myself a deadline to complete my major goals as quickly as possible. I also wanted to leave behind a legacy for my future kids. I've seen too many elderly people who had given up on their dreams; too many people with regrets. I didn't want to be another statistic. I pushed and pushed hard.

I actually accomplished my major goals at the age of thirty-eight. I'm not saying to take it to this extreme; however, this is your life and none of us know how much time we have. So use your time wisely and *abhor* waste.

Phrases to Help You Fear Failure

How many times have we heard this line, "I missed my goal's due date—it's no big deal—I'll just push the date out a few more months—I have too much going on right now." Try using some of these phrases to help instill a fear of failure.

❏ If I fail just one goal, I will fail all of my goals. I am tired of being a failure. I do not want to continue to be one for the rest of my life.

❏ Failure is unacceptable.

❏ I am running out of time.

❏ Next month I will be XX years old and I still keep pushing goal due dates further out—this pattern will continue until the day I die. I need to change now.

❏ When I die a picture will be placed on top of my casket and that will be the end of me. At the end of the ceremony—the only thing left will be that picture and memories. Leaving behind a legacy is just a pipe dream and will never become a reality unless I make it happen.

❏ Meeting a goal's due date is failure. I need to beat that date—always beat the due date.

Phrases and Tips to Help You Get Out of Bed Promptly

People have the most difficult time getting out of bed. Their minds will use all types of tricks to convince them to stay in that bed for just a few more minutes. Your internal saboteur will throw everything at you to derail your progress—trying to keep you in that bed longer. Try using some of the phrases below to get out of bed promptly.

❏ Another ten minutes adds up to hours of wasted time for the year.

❏ If you're exhausted, another ten minutes of sleep will not help.

❏ If I lounge around in bed today I will do the same thing tomorrow and the next day.

Excuse: I need to sleep a few extra hours—I don't want to feel tired later in the afternoon.

❏ It's all about how productive you can be now. We all get tired later in the day especially after a big lunch. You're always going to be more energetic and more creative at the beginning of your workday.

❏ If possible, take a quick power nap later in the day. Power naps are very effective. Just a quick snooze and you'll get a second wind.

❏ Do some sort of physical activity. Something light to get the blood flowing—I'm not talking a major workout.

- If you work from home, then get up from in front of that computer and clean something—perhaps the kitchen or organize your office. If you don't feel like cleaning—take a walk around the block.
- If you work in an office building, then get up and take a quick walk around the building—perhaps return some of your voicemails while walking to utilize your time efficiently. This serves several purposes: gets the blood flowing to wake you up and burns a few extra calories.

Excuse: Its cold outside—I don't want to get out of this warm bed to exercise.

❑ Simplify your morning routine. Go to bed with your clean workout clothes on. It's much easier than having to get up and change into your workout clothes especially when it's cold or raining outside.

❑ Set multiple alarm clocks. Keep one of them far away from the bed so you will have to get up to turn it off.

Phrases to Help You Instill a "Never Enough" Mentality

It feels great to accomplish a major goal. The first reaction is to tell yourself you need to take a long break... and that's certainly warranted—heck, you deserve it. But some of you may not want a break—although your mind and body are telling you otherwise. If you want to keep charging forward you may consider using some of these phrases:

❑ If I take one break I'll want to take more breaks. How badly do you want to leave behind a legacy? It's never going to happen if you take excessive time off.

❑ It's stupid to take a break now—I'll take a VERY long break when I die!

❑ Although I completed one of my major goals on time—I failed because I didn't complete it ahead of schedule.

❑ Accomplishing a few goals feels good—but it means nothing in the big scheme of things—go accomplish more.

Phrases and Tips to Help Manage Your Finances Effectively

When times are good, most businesses get lax when it comes

to managing expenses. The thinking is that the good times will continue forever. They only cut back when business takes a downturn due to a soft economy or fierce competition.

Proactively manage your finances

You should operate your business like the economy will crash any day. This doesn't mean you stop investing in necessary programs and functions—it just means maintaining a conservative budget. Be frugal throughout the year. It's a big mistake putting sound financial management practices on the back burner during the best of economic times. You need to be cost-conscious every day of the year. One of the stupidest things that businesses do is cut costs when there's a bad economy. They have layoffs, curtail spending and ask everyone to do more with less. Why wait until things go badly?

Surviving a potential layoff

Tell yourself repeatedly you will lose your job any day now. Even if times are good, they could change in a heartbeat—be prepared. This will force you to be cost-conscious throughout the year.

Establish a budget (document your expenditures)

Whether its grocery shopping or work related—evaluate all expenditures. Every time you go out to lunch, never look at spending ten dollars for lunch as it's only ten dollars. It adds up to at least five hundred dollars a year if you go out every week. You may consider that no big deal, but how many people actually only go out to lunch once a week? Don't go out more than once a week unless it's part of your job function.

Think of spending as a four-letter word—SAVE, SAVE, SAVE

Did you just spend an extra twelve dollars taking your wife to the movies in the evening instead of going to the Saturday afternoon matinee for half price? With the money you saved, you could take her to a few nice dinners or buy her a nice gift. Always extrapolate recurring expenses throughout the year.

Don't always buy the latest and greatest

Question yourself repeatedly. Do you really need to buy that item right now? You've survived without it all these years. The more you question yourself, the less likely you are to buy it, which means you probably didn't need it to begin with.

Phrases and Tips to Help You Save

Deposit something into your account consistently and frequently, preferably bi-monthly or monthly. If you have the option of depositing automatically through your company payroll deduction system, do so. If that option is not available, and you get paid bi-monthly, deposit funds into your savings account manually. You should also try to deposit extra funds, even if it's only a small amount. The key is to constantly watch your balance grow.

❏ Your mind will always want to look for more—but will never be satisfied.

❏ Eventually your mind will get bored at looking at the same number and will always force you to deposit more. It's a major sense of accomplishment to see that number increase frequently. The more frequent the better—your mind will be trained to anticipate a growing balance.

❏ Try and beat your own savings goals. Tell yourself repeatedly "I NEED TO BEAT THAT NUMBER." Even if it's only by a few dollars.

❏ You can NEVER withdraw money from your savings account. If you withdraw funds one time you will want to do it again and again. Have a hands-off policy. Your savings are only for major purchases (e.g., home) or for a major emergency (e.g., loss of employment).

Plan ahead

Establish realistic savings goals for six months, one year and beyond..

Equate money to your career or business

❏ Typically the more you make the more successful you are. Making money is your top priority—say it dozens of times each day! MONEY, MONEY, MONEY. Tell yourself repeatedly that the world revolves around money.

Redirecting Negative Emotions

I used some hardcore phrases to combat negative emotions. These phrases were used to train my mind to redirect negativity into a powerful force of positive energy. This energy allowed me to focus on my priorities and daily milestones. My trained mind put up a barrier to protect me from those negative feelings. Those feelings of depression were not going to keep me down for very long.

Some of the phrases I used may work for you, or you may want to come up with your own. You need to find the phrases that will have the most impact on you—if they're not on the following lists, come up with your own.

The phrases I used to redirect my negative emotions were very hardcore (mean and nasty). I used these phrases to move the negativity aside and thrust me forward to focus solely on my daily milestones. This was an *internal* struggle only. The more hardcore these phrases were, the less time I spent thinking about the negativity and the more I spent on being positive and living life with urgency.

Phrases to Help Redirect Negative Emotions
Example #1

I had a very difficult breakup in my late twenties. It was someone who I loved very much. When we separated I was distraught. I lost focus, energy and motivation. Within a few hours I was back to normal again because of a few very nasty phrases I said to myself repeatedly: *she's a loser, she's a piece of... She's probably with some other guy right now; she's not worth it....* In other words, I trashed her in my mind. Did I really feel that way? No way. However, my trained mind made me believe she was a bad person—that's all it took! The objective is not to look back and dwell on the past. It's over, put things behind you and focus on the future. Life must go on—the sooner the better.

Example #2

I had a close friend (at least I thought I did) who I treated like a brother. I provided him with continuous support (personal advice, business support and financial help upon request). My friend had a lot of great qualities, but managing his finances effectively wasn't one of them. I lent him more than $100,000 over ten years. A promissory note was written and signed by both parties with each loan. In the end the promissory notes were worthless. He never paid back a dollar—he defaulted on the loans.

A lawsuit ensued and judgment was awarded to me. I was very upset and hurt—I couldn't believe that someone who I treated better than my own brother would burn me in this manner.

My trained mind redirected my negative emotions into my priorities by having me believe that he was a loser—it got me back on track quickly. I used phrases like: *he is nothing but a piece of... he's a loser...* Did I really feel this way about my close friend so quickly? Of course not/ I still cared for him very much. I blamed myself too because I knew about his financial management shortcomings. Regardless of how you feel, use key phrases that will get you angry enough to redirect those negative emotions into *powerful positive energy*. The key is to get back on track quickly.

I am happy to report that after several years of not speaking to my old friend, he reached out to me and began making amends—he sends me a percentage of his income every month. I forgave him— after all we are all human and we all make mistakes. Our friendship continues to flourish.

Dealing with emotional conflict is probably the hardest challenges you will face. It is extremely difficult to hold yourself accountable when you are dealing with these sorts of setbacks. They are the biggest time wasters of all.

Be prepared—bad situations WILL happen. When they do, know the phrases you want to use and start repeating them over and over and over again until your mind takes over and leads you forward. Let's say you get into a big fight with your significant other—you're in a bad mood and you don't feel like doing anything. You may want to try the phrases below to snap out of it.

- ❏ Precious minutes are being wasted—you're a fool to let this stupid fight drag on.
- ❏ The argument is over—stop dwelling on it—it gets you nowhere.
- ❏ You can't win—who cares who wins—it's irrelevant—give in— you have more important things to do.
- ❏ Step back and take a deep breath—do not be confrontational.
- ❏ She's a wonderful person—don't be stupid.

Repeating phrases to train your mind may sound a bit weird, but it's the best way to keep yourself on top of your goals. You need to determine which phrases leave their mark and cause you to change, redirect and stay focused on your priorities and milestones. Remember, your objective is to get on with your life as quickly as possible, not to wallow in depression.

Using negative phrases to redirect negative emotions may seem contradictory, but they are very effective. The nastier the situation, the more challenging it will be to train your mind. In these situations you need hardcore methods to stay on track toward a more productive life.

Be Repetitive

How do you get there? How do you *train your mind* to push yourself to achieve your daily milestones? One word: *repetition.* It's not rocket science—it's simple and very basic, however it must be practiced properly and consistently.

Pretend you're a drill sergeant. Get tough on yourself.

You are training your mind to stay focused on the task at hand. An untrained mind comes up with ways to bedevil you and sabotage your best efforts. It is no fun to be a battlefield within—one part of you working desperately to achieve your goals, the other part of you missing vital appointments, using inappropriate language, engaging in addictive behaviors and so on. There's only one way to hold yourself accountable to your priorities, goals and daily milestones, and that's to train your mind to do so automatically.

The value of training your mind and the necessity of it will nudge you forward even when your body is feeling tired and a part of you just wants to be lazy. By training your mind, you are taking control of your inner world.

The Man in the Mirror

Without a doubt the secret to holding yourself accountable is to train your mind. A simplified version that I used for years is what I refer to as the Man-In-The-Mirror (MIM) technique. The MIM technique is a very simple concept of conversing with yourself repeatedly, which automates your mind into taking control of your actions. I need to reemphasize that it's the man in the mirror because accountability is on you.

Once trained, your mind behaves like your own personal drill sergeant. This drill sergeant will combat inefficient use of time and automatically motivate you every day. A good drill sergeant is firm and determined. He doesn't accept excuses. He pushes for the end result.

The conversations you have with yourself are unique to you. You can make them funny or military-like. The idea is for you to take control of your inner world and you are the one taking control. Only you know what motivates you. In order to play the mind game properly, you need to know what the benefit is and also what you fear.

Treat Every Day Equally

Treating every day equally means just that. One of the best ways to train your mind to hold yourself accountable is to be consistent. Below is a process flow diagram on how to treat every day equally.

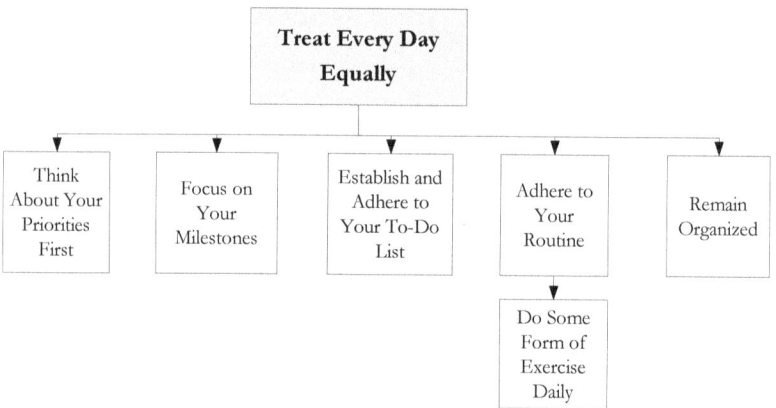

How can every day be treated the same? What about holidays and weekends? It would be ludicrous to put forth the same effort seven days a week—everyone needs a break to recharge. Besides, I'm not suggesting you be a workaholic seven days a week just focus on your priorities first every day.

What if you don't want to do anything on Sundays but relax and watch TV? It's simple—just *plan ahead* and put a bit more effort into your priorities throughout the week or on Saturday. Don't just live your week by the seat of your pants—plan it out thoroughly. Be productive with your time and utilize every minute so then you can feel totally free to goof off and have fun.

Avoiding Temptations

Temptations are all around us. It's challenging, to say the least, to do what's right instead of doing what's much more fun and exciting:

- ❏ When you're at a bar with friends and everyone is drinking up a storm, except you, this means limiting the amount of alcohol you consume so you can remain in control.
- ❏ Avoiding places that invite bad temptations, like going to a bar without your spouse. I'm not saying something bad will happen, but why even go there and put yourself in that type of setting, where the temptation is so great.
- ❏ If you're married—if, say, you travel on business trips—the temptations on the road are great. You may feel the urge to go out looking for fun instead of staying in your hotel room and getting some work done or watching a movie.
- ❏ If you're trying to reduce the amount of junk food you consume, don't go to fast food restaurants with your colleagues or friends. Why place yourself in that environment?

Summary

Look at the people around you, the ones who are unsuccessful, just surviving. Is that who you want to become? Mastering your life is hard work, that's why only very few people become successful. How badly do you want success? It means devoting an extraordinary amount of resources to achieve this feat. The most difficult aspect of achieving personal and professional excellence is consistently holding yourself accountable. In this section I educated you on how to:

- ❏ Establish a contract with yourself (rules and guidelines)

You *will* remain structured, abide by your priorities, manage time effectively, maintain values and spend quality time with your family or loved one.

- ❏ Establish phrases

These phrases will be used to train your mind. They must be meaningful and impactful to cause positive change in your life. They are phrases that will be used to alter the way you operate every day. Be repetitive (with those phrases) to begin training your mind.

- ❏ Train your mind

Treat every day equally

- Remain organized (home, office, email)
- Follow a routine
- Adhere to a to-do list
❏ Become your own cop—hold yourself accountable every day

There is only one way to hold yourself accountable consistently and that's to train your mind to do it for you automatically. Training your mind is the key to success. Having a trained mind to accomplish whatever your heart desires is like no other feeling. In the next section I share with you its benefits.

The End Result

Being responsible for your actions consistently is exactly the characteristic you want to have in life. You will actually feel superhuman. That may sound like an exaggeration, but it's how I actually feel every day. I'm on top of the world—bring it on! I have mastered my life and I feel awesome. I have the confidence to take it all on and then some. I'm not being egotistical—just being very confident in my capabilities.

With your mind trained, you will be resistant to failure. You will not take a long fall after a major breakup with your significant other. You will no longer waste time and you will achieve all of your goals. Below is a process flow of what the end result looks like.

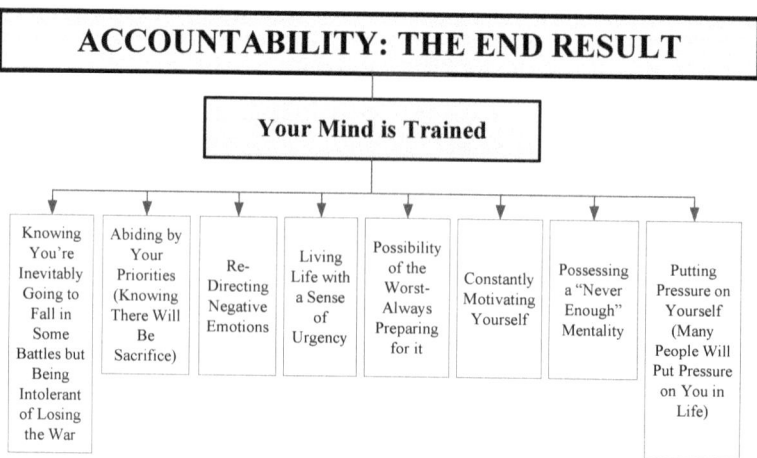

Your Mind is Trained

When my mind was trained, I knew it. I was 'robot-like' in everything I did. I was in one mode every day of the week. I was on a mission. My mission was to accomplish, accomplish and accomplish more. One accomplishment or several accomplishments meant nothing to me. Sure, I was excited—maybe for an hour or two, but then it was on to another goal and eventually another accomplishment. I trained my mind so much that the biggest turn-on were those accomplishments. Once trained, the mind will act as a guiding, calculating tool that will provide you with immense benefits.

- ❏ You will make decisions more readily and be more committed to them.
- ❏ You will be extremely focused.
- ❏ You will readily manage your projects, tasks and obligations more effectively and with more dexterity.
- ❏ You will possess a sense of urgency.
- ❏ You will always abide by your priorities.
- ❏ You will always be motivated.
- ❏ You will always be held accountable.

The process to train your mind is easy—it's not rocket science. It is a closely-followed system of reminders that is used to keep you focused on your commitments. Think of it as a bridge between being disciplined and not. Furthermore, consider it as merely obtaining a necessary mental state, much like a degree or a certificate. Once completed, it will make your journey towards self-mastery more realistic and rewarding.

Once your mind is trained, the execution is automatic because the mind takes over and adheres to your priorities. The mind is set to autopilot. You cannot disengage from the autopilot—your mind won't let you. It is now controlling your body as it does mine every day.

How Will You Know?

What does it take to be motivated every day of the year and be able to hold yourself accountable to your to-do list and milestones?

- ❏ You won't be able to lounge in bed and do nothing
- ❏ That wonderful sense of accomplishment becomes addictive

❏ You will treat every day equally

❏ You're actually scared to death to revert back to your old ways

❏ You won't be able to make excuses

Summary

In this step you learned what accountability is, how you attain it and what the end result means to you. The only way to consistently hold yourself accountable is to train your mind to do so automatically.

When you hold yourself accountable every day of the year you will have instilled the ultimate level of discipline into your life. You will be able to accomplish anything. Your mentality is at a different level. You will have an abundance of confidence. You will be structured, live by your priorities and manage time efficiently.

You will feel superhuman. Congratulations, being responsible for your actions and commitments is the level everyone wants to be at! To accomplish *every* one of your goals is a feeling that's second to none! You will:

❏ Live life with a sense of urgency

❏ Constantly be motivated

❏ Redirect negative emotions into a powerful positive force of energy

❏ Possess a *never enough* mentality

❏ Be intolerant of failing the war—although you may lose some battles

❏ Constantly put pressure on yourself to produce at a higher level—no outside pressure or obstacle will stress you out

❏ Be healthy and energetic

❏ Maintain values

❏ Never become complacent

❏ Be proactive to ensure you live a balanced lifestyle

❏ Be happy

❏ Now that you are disciplined you will always want more: to be healthier, own more property, go on more vacations and help others

❏ You won't be able to stop—have fun with it

STEP 5: SEEK PERFECTION

You won't be able to stop now. You're disciplined! You'll want to get physically and mentally stronger. You'll want to be more productive and accomplish more. One of the most effective ways to continue to grow is by monitoring, assessing and rating your progress daily. It only takes a few minutes. The rewards can be substantial. It's not enough to be productive occasionally: you need to seek perfection every day.

Never Be Satisfied

"Look at a day when you are supremely satisfied at the end. It's not a day when you lounge around doing nothing; it's when you've had everything to do, and you've done it."
Lord Acton

Life is all about accomplishments; The more you accomplish, one thing after another, the happier you become. What a rush, like no other feeling. Those are *real* highs. It's a self-inflicted adrenaline rush you can't get it out of your system once you've experienced it. The more you accomplish, the more you crave accomplishments for yourself. You will *never* be satisfied. What a feeling it is to always want more, take on new challenges and accomplish more year after year. Life now has purpose.

I can't imagine not accomplishing one goal after another until the day I drop. If there are no accomplishments, there is no life, or at best, it's an unfulfilled life. There is no purpose for living. You may exist, but that's not living. Living is progressing, not merely breathing.

"To live is so startling it leaves little time for anything else."
Emily Dickinson

There is no greater feeling in the world than accomplishing a major goal. Once you complete a goal, you will never forget it. It's hard to describe in mere words what the feeling is like. It's a kind of euphoria that not only makes you feel invincible, but it is extremely addictive as well. The level of intensity is relative to the difficulty of the goal. The harder the goal, the stronger the feeling of accomplishment will be. You can take my word for it. I still remember each and every goal, even the ones I accomplished many years ago.

The secret is to stay hungry and never be completely satisfied. The best thing you can do is to keep piling up those tasks as long as they're meaningful. The more tasks you have on your plate, the hungrier you will be and complete satisfaction will be a figment of your imagination.

The true measure of a person's success and happiness is their emotional, physical and psychological well-being. Never be satisfied with the level of happiness you've attained. There are always areas in our lives that need attention to keep the balance consistent. Being happy in all aspects of your life is the mother of all accomplishments. Don't settle. If you must, remember to always settle for more. Below is a process flow on how to continuously seek perfection.

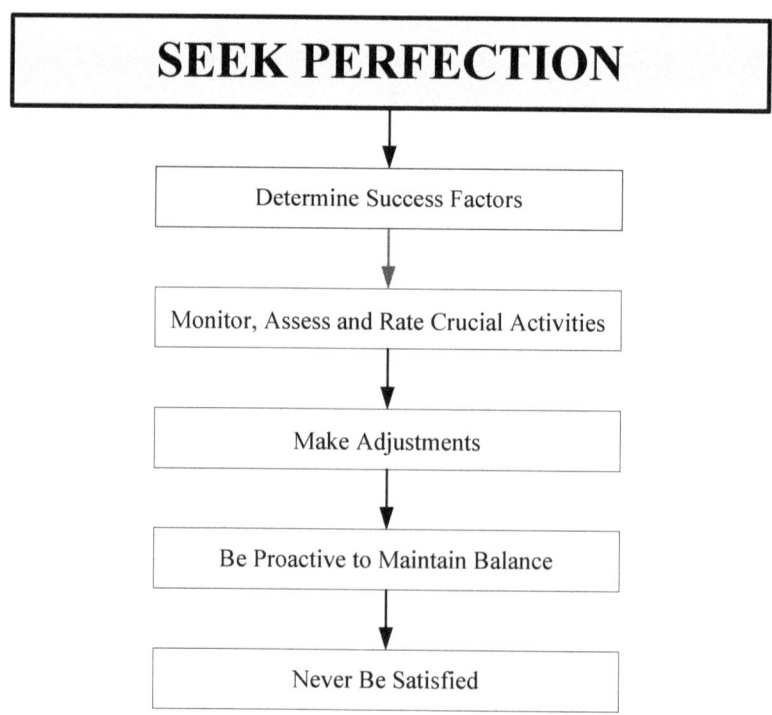

Determine Success Factors and Criteria

What constitutes success for you? Let's look at one of my key success factors. My exercise routine is crucial to get my day started off on the right track. It begins each morning between 3 and 4 AM and lasts an hour or more. A good workout would mean:

- ❏ I felt mentally ready to exercise
- ❏ My legs felt strong during my cardiovascular workout and I burned 250 or more calories
- ❏ I stretched
- ❏ I left the gym with a good (muscular) pump
- ❏ I felt energetic
- ❏ No injuries
- ❏ I was very focused—there were no distractions
- ❏ For me the above criteria constitutes a good workout. Pick the indicators that are the most relevant for you.

Monitor, Assess, and Rate Success Factors

Take a snapshot of your productivity every day—a simple rating system will suffice. Determine the most important criteria for each success factor. Which criteria will help you achieve success fastest? If maintaining good health is one of your most important success factors, your criteria could be a quality exercise routine, eating right, a good cardiovascular workout and limited socializing.

What will it take to make you successful in your *career*, *health* and *relationships*? My success factors are based on key criteria and associating up to 5 points for each. Rate each area on a scale of 1-5 (5 being excellent). Then add them up and divide by the number of success factors to determine your score for the day. My goal is to achieve a score of 4.0 or above every day.

Harris Kern's Success Factors

Success Factors	Criteria	Rating
Focusing on priorities	No deviation	5
Sleep optimally (less than 5 hours)	Get out of bed promptly	5
	Getting to bed on time	
Quality exercise routine	Stay focused	5
	Stay energetic	
	Don't socialize	
	Don't take shortcuts	
Maintain structure	Manage your email inbox	4
	Keep the office organized	
	Ensure a to-do list is created each evening	
	Lay out clothes the night before	
	Keep the home organized and clean	
Spend a minimum of one hour of quality time with family		3
Cook a healthy dinner for the family		4
Spend a minimum of one hour writing content for the latest book		4
Update all client action plans		3
Manage time efficiently		4
Average Score		4.1

The rating process is somewhat subjective because you determine what your 5 equates to. Assess all success factors that you feel fall below a score of 4 closely. For example, why did I rate myself a 3 when it came to updating client action plans in the table above?

❏ Did I lose focus—if so why?

❏ Was I lazy?

❏ Did I have too many interruptions throughout the day?

❏ Did I put it off until the end of the day? After all, it is administrative work and not very exciting.

Never stop trying to master *every* aspect of your life. Keep asking yourself questions—keep strategizing to achieve greatness—keep seeking perfection.

Make Adjustments

For success factors that are scored a 3 or below, make the appropriate adjustments. *Whatever the reason, what am I going to do differently next time to be more efficient in this area? Maybe I need to make adjustments in my routine. Maybe there's too much I'm trying to accomplish on any given day.*

For example, if you're always starving during your workout and it's affecting the quality of this success factor, shift your daily routine around or eat something light before exercising.

What are your success factors? Rate yourself on that activity daily, but don't do it haphazardly or occasionally. Life changes constantly—it's important to make adjustments to keep on top of it all. Your priorities won't change but your routine may. Do whatever it takes to become more efficient.

Be Proactive

Constantly being proactive is critical in reaching the ultimate level of personal mastery. Stay on top of your success factors at all times. Don't get complacent and assume you're doing well. Proactively gauging progress ensures that you're not only being efficient but it also allows you to maintain that balanced lifestyle we all seek. The more efficient you are, the more balanced your life will become. You will have more time to enjoy the things you love doing.

My way of life is exciting, challenging and balanced for me. I enjoyed getting little sleep, exercising daily, traveling with my family, growing my business, helping people and having *many* accomplishments. For others it could be different, but remember that in order to maintain balance, you need to proactively monitor your success factors daily. It's easy to put too much emphasis into any one activity; however, with proactive monitoring you will be able to allocate your resources appropriately, for all of your most important activities. This will allow you to maintain that balanced lifestyle you desire.

As noted earlier; you won't be able to stop. You'll want to get physically and mentally stronger. You'll want to be more productive and accomplish more. One of the most effective ways to continue to grow is by monitoring, rating and assessing your progress daily. It only takes a few minutes.

Maintain Balance

Yes, it's an old cliché, but so true! Maintaining balance is easier said than done. I learned dearly from mistakes. I invested so much time in my career and maintaining excellent health that at times I put family on the back burner. This wasn't done intentionally, nor did I mean to hurt anyone—I loved my family. But I had to make adjustments quickly. I started assessing and rating my key success factors. If I was monitoring my activities from the beginning I would have seen that all of my resources were consumed by two of my priorities.

Summary

No one is perfect and no one will ever be perfect—that's a guarantee! So why am I telling you to seek perfection? Because everyone should always try to improve especially in the *big three* areas of life: *career, health* and *relationships.* Wouldn't you want more promotions at work? Don't you want to be healthier—more energetic, with more stamina? Wouldn't you always want your relationships to be more meaningful?

As far as I know, you will be on this planet one time. No one has been able to prove otherwise—so why not go for the gusto? If you're now disciplined then you will *never* be satisfied—just like me. You'll constantly want to improve in *every* aspect of your life. Especially with the big three priorities—career, health and relationships.

In this section you learned to choose your success factors, the activities that constitute success for you. Once you determine those activities, select the criteria that should be monitored, assessed and rated daily. If you have a high rating, congratulations. If you have a poor rating make adjustments; change your routine. A quality exercise routine is critical to maintain balance. Being proactive and gauging progress will promote success.

❏ Determine success factors

What are your most important activities? Which ones will help you achieve success?

❏ Determine criteria for each activity

Let's say that maintaining good health was one of your most important activities. The criteria could be eating right that day, getting to the gym on time, not socializing at the gym, burning a lot of calories and being very energetic. Pick the criteria that make sense for you and score your health related activity based on the criteria.

❑ Rate the efficiency of each success factor

On a scale of 1-5 rate your efficiency.

❑ Make adjustments if applicable

For success factors that score below a 4, make the appropriate adjustments.

❑ Be proactive to maintain balance

One of the main reasons to rate yourself is to maintain a good, balanced lifestyle. It's easy to put too much emphasis on any one priority; however, by being proactive and monitoring yourself daily, you will be able to maintain that balanced lifestyle we all seek.

Life has two parts: Being successful while you're alive and being remembered when you're dead. While you're alive, adopt discipline and you will automatically leave behind a legacy.

PART III: THE PROOF

INDIVIDUAL CASE STUDIES

I've been mentoring people and organizations in the areas of personal and professional growth for over thirty years. I thought you might find it interesting to see the transformation someone goes through when my five steps are applied to develop their self-discipline skills.

These are all real people. First I give you the background of the person I'm mentoring and their problems from my perspective. I then tell you the action steps I came up with after the initial evaluation. The last part is the results, the after. Perhaps you'll see yourself in one of these case studies.

Spends More than She Makes

Grace is a single mother with two kids who lives and works in San Francisco. She worked very hard and rewarded herself by taking several vacations a year. The price tag was fairly high. Although she barely made enough to pay her bills, she felt that vacations were a necessity. I totally agree that vacations are important, but only if you have the money to pay for them.

Her vacations were paid for by credit card—incurring more debt every year. Typically, the first few weeks after returning from a vacation, she felt great—stress-free. However, once she received her credit card bill and digested the new balance, it didn't take long for the stress to return. Were the vacations really worth it?

Grace lived for today and rarely thought about the future. She didn't want to sacrifice her vacations for long-term benefits. After a several years the debt became enormous. She called and asked me if I could help. I said yes, but I also told her there wasn't an easy and painless fix. I also told her that she would have to make some wholesale sacrifices in her life. Below is a synopsis of my mentoring process with Grace.

Action Taken	
1	I facilitated an assessment of Grace's life. The first step was to thoroughly understand her strengths, weaknesses and her personal and professional goals. Once I completed the assessment, we reviewed my findings and discussed a strategy going forward.
2	Before proceeding, we had a heart-to-heart discussion. I told her this wasn't going to be easy and that based on her issues, my mentoring program could take one year or longer. "Your biggest challenge will be to live within a budget. If you don't think you can change your ways, let's not proceed. I don't want to waste my time or yours."
3	We established one priority: finances. Her family would always get top billing, but that was the easy part.
4	I began developing her self-discipline skills. The mentoring was based on the five steps discussed throughout this book: 1. Instituting Structure: Adhering to her new budget. 2. Prioritizing One's Life: Finances were the primary focus. 3. Managing Time: She had horrible time management practices. She wasted a good five hours a day. 4. Holding Oneself Accountable: I trained her mind to eventually hold herself accountable by using phrases which impacted her. 5. Seeking Perfection: Once we had her mind trained to adhere to a budget she wanted to continue to strive for excellence. We established more challenging goals.
5	I designed a strategy to manage her finances effectively. This included: • Eliminating credit card debt. • Opening a savings account. • Requesting access to her bank records to monitor expenditures daily. • Planning her monthly billing cycle, forecasting future purchases, which included inexpensive vacations. • Putting large expenditures off limits, leaving only necessities (food, utilities and clothes for the kids).
6	I developed a roadmap with financial goals and milestones. One of her milestones was to deposit a minimum of twenty dollars every week into a savings account.
7	I had Grace establish a to-do list every evening.
8	I trained her mind to think differently about expenditures. I instructed her to extrapolate expenditures for the year, not just for that day. She was spending two thousand dollars a year on lunch.
9	I reviewed her bank statements together each month.
10	I held her accountable to her to-do list and budget daily
11	I trained her mind to hold herself accountable.
12	I had weekly (typically Saturday or Sunday) conversations to discuss progress and strategize on ways to continuously improve.
Results	
1	She eliminated her credit card debt.

2	After three months she increased her monthly savings deposit to twenty five dollars and after six months she increased it to forty dollars. She actually enjoyed watching her savings grow.
3	She brought her lunch to work daily.
4	After her credit card debt was eliminated, she was still working on eliminating her student loans, which was the bulk of her debt.
5	She lived within a budget.
6	Eventually she was able to hold herself accountable for her actions.

The Yes-Man

Jason couldn't say no to anyone—he was just too nice of a guy, a yes-man. Unfortunately he rarely had the time to focus on his goals: home ownership, substantial savings, consistent exercise and excelling in his career.

One of Jason's good friends was remodeling his home. He asked Jason to come by after work one night to help for a few hours. It started out being one night a week and quickly grew to three nights a week. It was a wonderful gesture. Unfortunately, it was hard work and it was burning Jason out. He was exhausted during the day which hurt his creativity and productivity at work.

Can you honestly guarantee that your friends will be in your life ten years from now? The odds aren't good. In the end his friend had a newly remodeled home. Jason still had an apartment, had no savings account and was still not going anywhere in his career.

Action Taken	
1	I facilitated an assessment of Jason's life. The first step was to understand his strengths, weaknesses and goals. Once I completed my fact-finding exercise, we reviewed the results and discussed a strategy to move forward.
2	We determined that his top priorities should be career, health and relationships. I told him that these are all top priorities. However, the priority of relationships rarely means spending twenty hours a week helping a friend remodel his home. After family and perhaps God there are very few cycles left for friends. It's unfortunate but it's reality. To be successful, Jason needed to help himself first. I also told him that once he gets disciplined he can spend more time helping his friends.
3	Jason started developing his self-discipline skills using the five steps discussed throughout this book.
4	He developed a roadmap with new goals, milestones and a daily routine based on his priorities. If time permitted, he could help his friend periodically (a few days a month—if possible). Even if it was one day a month, Jason's friend would still be grateful. Wouldn't you be? Friends will not think any less of friends who help out when they can.

5	We established a to-do list each evening.
6	We trained Jason's mind to treat every day equally.
7	I mentored Jason on how to be a nice jerk. He learned how to say no to people in the appropriate manner.
8	I held him accountable to the tasks on his to-do list several times a day via telephone calls, text and email.
9	We had weekly (typically Saturday or Sunday) conversations to discuss progress and strategize on ways to continuously improve.
Results	
1	Jason was eventually promoted at work.
2	He used his time wisely and lived by his priorities—they always came first.
3	He learned to effectively say no.
4	He exercised consistently.
5	He purchased his first home after a few years.
6	Eventually, he held himself accountable for his actions.

Family Obligations Preventing Success

Bill was a single man in his early thirties. He lived in an apartment and had a good job. But he felt like he never had enough time to focus on his goals. He was spending half of his resources (time and money) on family matters (e.g., financial assistance, personal errands, family get-togethers or frequent and lengthy phone calls—listening to everyone's problems). His brothers, sisters, cousins, father and mother all depended on him.

Bill had to manage his family's financial matters. His dad was living overseas and Bill was paying his living expenses. Bill was also helping his mother who lived in a nearby apartment. This generosity was very honorable, but he failed miserably with his finances. He was barely getting by—living day-to-day with no savings. Bill was an excellent real estate agent—when times were good, his income soared. But when business slowed and the income dried up, it was too late because he had spent it all helping his family.

It was only a matter of time until the bills started piling up and everything around him would come crashing down. In the end, he lost and his family lost too. He went into debt. Creditors were calling, he was about to be evicted and lenders were about ready to repossess his car. Bill failed miserably. That's when he contacted me.

His major goal was to buy a home in the next five years. We

needed to make some wholesale changes in the way he allocated time and managed his finances.

Action Taken	
1	I facilitated an evaluation to understand Bill's strengths, weaknesses and goals. Part of the evaluation was to analyze his daily routine. The amount of time being allocated to his family was truly eye-opening. Once I completed my fact-finding exercise, we reviewed the results and discussed a strategy to move forward.
2	I made it clear to Bill that he would have to make some major sacrifices to achieve his goals. One of the areas would be spending less time dealing with family issues. Three-quarters of his time was used by his family. We agreed to reduce it to twenty-five percent. The remaining time would be dedicated to his priorities. At the end of the day he needed to make himself less available.
3	I designed a strategy based on his goals and two new priorities: career and finances. The strategy also included developing his self-discipline skills based on the five steps discussed in this book.
4	We developed a roadmap with realistic goals, milestones and a new routine.
5	Most if not all non-work-related phone calls were sent to his voicemail. If it wasn't an emergency, he would call back the next day or later that evening. If certain calls required immediate attention, conversations were limited to ten minutes. He learned to cut people off politely, with excuses and little white lies where necessary. I assured him that his family would still love him. He was still there for them (just not as much). In the long run his family would be better off financially. If Bill was successful with his career, everyone would win. If he continued down the same path, everyone would lose.
6	I had Bill establish and email me a to-do list each evening.
7	I held Bill accountable to his to-do list and routine several times throughout the day (once via email, several text messages and one quick phone call).
8	I trained Bill's mind by treating every day equally, and had him repeat key phrases.
9	We had weekly (typically Saturday or Sunday) conversations to discuss progress and strategize on ways to continuously improve.
Results	
1	Bill started a savings account—his nest egg was growing nicely. In a few years he will have enough money to make a down payment on a home.
2	Bill spent minimal time taking care of others; he was focusing resources on his career.
3	Bill was promoted to a management position.
4	Eventually Bill's mind was trained and he was able to hold himself accountable for his actions.

Excelled in her Career but Failed Miserably in her Personal Life

Anne is a genius. She received an MBA from USC by the age of twenty-two. She was a successful attorney before the age of twenty-seven. She was dealing in corporate acquisitions and mergers—earning around $400,000 a year. She focused all of her time on her career. She came to me on her fortieth birthday requesting assistance. She wanted balance in her life. She also wanted to lose forty pounds—and keep it off.

Anne had completely ignored her personal life. She was working seven days a week. She was overweight, eating junk food every night. She traveled feverishly. She never had a relationship and never exercised. Her health was deteriorating and her personal life was nonexistent. The challenge was to prescribe a formula that would allocate enough cycles to focus on her personal life, but also not diminish the drive and passion for her career.

She thrived on the pressures of her career. She loved her job—you could hear the passion in her voice when she described what she did. It's what turned her on. Although Anne was averaging fourteen-hour workdays for the past fifteen years, burnout was not an issue—she *thrived* on pressure.

Action Taken	
1	I facilitated an assessment of Anne's life. The first step was to thoroughly understand her strengths, weaknesses and personal and professional goals. Once I completed the assessment, we reviewed my findings and discussed a strategy to move forward.
2	I monitored her current routine, including the days she traveled, and found that there was ample time she could devote to exercise.
3	I designed a strategy to focus on two priorities: career and health. Her career goals were easy—nothing changed—we just needed to incorporate health-related goals into her work schedule. She wanted to manage her food intake and exercise consistently.
4	We started developing her self-discipline skills using the five steps discussed throughout this book. Everything to do with her professional life was exemplary. However, everything to do with her personal life was a mess. We established a routine that would keep her personal life organized.
5	I had Anne establish a to-do list each evening, which included her personal milestones, errands and obligations.
6	I documented a roadmap with health-related milestones. The roadmap also had triggers to help her maintain structure.

7	Anne committed two days a week for exercise and, on the weeks she wasn't traveling, exercised four days a week.
8	I trained her mind by having her treat every day equally, which included adhering to her routine and following her to-do list faithfully.
9	I adjusted her eating habits. At times junk food couldn't be avoided, but on other occasions where it could, she would snack on nuts and fruit. The objective was to help her develop the same passion for health as she had for her career.
10	I trained her mind to live life with a sense of urgency when it came to her health. We used phrases that grossed her out (e.g., constantly thinking about herself in a bathing suit while she was 40 pounds overweight).
11	I held her accountable to her milestones every day via email, text and phone calls.
12	We had weekly (typically Saturday or Sunday) conversations to discuss progress and strategize on ways to continuously improve.
Results	
1	Anne lost forty pounds, and kept it off.
2	She ate much healthier.
3	She consistently exercised.
4	She was more energetic and had more stamina.
5	She improved the quality of her sleep.
6	Eventually, Anne's mind was trained and she was able to hold herself accountable for her health-related activities.

Career Stalled

Sam was thirty-seven, married, making approximately $45,000 a year as a line manager for a large retail firm. He was frustrated because his career had stalled—he hadn't been promoted in four years.

Sam contacted me because he felt like he never had time to complete his projects. He also felt that he was scatterbrained—constantly losing focus. Sam also had weak management skills: he was an ineffective communicator, didn't manage key relationships and was disorganized.

Action Taken	
1	I facilitated an assessment of Sam's life. The first step was to understand his strengths, weaknesses and goals. Once I completed my fact-finding process we reviewed the results and discussed a strategy to move forward.
2	I established one priority for Sam: his career.

3	I designed a strategy to help Sam focus on his career. Included in the strategy were specific goals to develop Sam's leadership skills.
4	I started developing his self-discipline skills using the five steps discussed throughout this book.
5	I developed a roadmap with realistic goals and specific career-related milestones.
6	I established a new routine based on his new priority. The routine would help keep him focused on his career-related milestones.
7	I mentored Sam on how to maintain structure: • Established a to-do list each evening and followed it daily. I held him accountable throughout the day. • Picked out his work clothes the night before. • Had him keep his email, home and work environment organized. • Held him accountable to his new routine.
8	I developed his management/leadership skills.
9	I trained Sam's mind by having him treat every day equally. I also had him repeat key phrases that impacted him in a positive manner.
10	We held him accountable to his to-do list every day via telephone calls, texting and email.
11	I had weekly (typically Saturday or Sunday) conversations to discuss progress and strategize on ways to continuously improve.
Results	
1	Sam managed time effectively.
2	Sam became much more productive by maintaining structure throughout the day.
3	Sam was eventually promoted to a higher management position.
4	Sam eventually was able to hold himself accountable for his actions.

Living Beyond His Means

Dan was thirty-four and living with his girlfriend in a one bedroom apartment. His salary was about $60,000. She was making about $35,000. Although Dan wanted to excel in his career and make more money, he didn't want to invest the extra effort. He would rather work exactly eight hours and spend every additional minute with his girlfriend.

Both were in debt and living beyond their means. Their credit cards were maxed out. Dan still wanted to marry his sweetheart. He also wanted to buy her an expensive engagement ring (on credit of course) and buy her a new car (on credit).

I facilitated a formal evaluation. He sorely lacked any sort of discipline. His financial situation was ugly yet he didn't want to face reality. I told him that he had to make sacrifices in his life or I wouldn't proceed. I knew that this fantasy world they were living in would eventually crash on them.

Action Taken	
1	I wished him luck on his future wedding and said goodbye. It's easy to get married, but the challenge is staying married when you have a shaky career and you're in severe debt. How long do you honestly think he will be living in paradise? You cannot be successful over the long haul without initially making sacrifices.

The Alcoholic

Carlos was fifty-two and married to his high school sweetheart. Carlos and his wife are both alcoholics. Unfortunately Carlos has been arrested for DUI and ordered to attend Alcoholics Anonymous. It didn't work—he was still drinking. The years of drinking also took a toll on his motivation and overall productivity at work. His health deteriorated considerably: he was sick frequently, he rarely had energy and was almost fired from his job—he actually received a written warning. That's when he decided to contact me.

Action Taken	
1	I facilitated an assessment of Carlos. The first step was to understand his strengths, weaknesses and goals. Once I completed my fact-finding exercise, we reviewed the results and discussed a strategy to move forward.
2	I established two priorities: career and health.
3	I designed a strategy to accomplish his goals based on his two new priorities.
4	I developed a roadmap with realistic goals, milestones and one routine for Monday—Friday and one routine for the weekend per his request.
5	I started developing his self-discipline skills using the five steps discussed throughout this book.
6	I had Carlos prepare a to-do list each night before going to bed. He would email me a copy. This included the weekend.
7	I trained his mind to treat every day equally by focusing on his milestones, routine and to-do list first each day.
8	I had him maintain structure throughout the day, such as organize desk each evening before leaving the office, maintain email inbox, update to-do list.
9	Continuously reminded him that it was now or never—if he received another DUI he could go to jail and his license would be taken away for a long time. He could also seriously hurt or kill someone.

10	I held Carlos accountable daily (yes, including weekends) via telephone calls, text and email. We discussed his milestones, progress or lack thereof, what worked and what didn't work.
11	I documented his progress in an Excel spreadsheet. This included tracking the number of consecutive days he went without drinking.
12	We had weekly (typically Saturday or Sunday) conversations to discuss progress and strategize on ways to continuously improve.
Results	
1	Carlos is now consistently productive every day.
2	He hasn't taken a drink in a year.
3	He exercises five days a week.
4	He's excelling in his career— he's actually now a successful salesman.
5	He holds himself accountable for his actions.

Mr. Emotions

Tom was thirty-seven, and married with no kids. He was a salesman earning approximately $75,000 a year. He earned his income solely on commission. If he was organized and followed a strict routine and focused on his goals he could have earned four times that amount. Unfortunately, Tom was not. He would always lose focus because of constant issues in his personal life. If something negative happened the night before, those negative vibes would hang around the next day and his productivity would suffer greatly. He would actually shut down and call it a day.

When he had issues, he didn't produce—unfortunately when he didn't produce he had *more* issues due to his financial situation—he couldn't pay his bills. His priority was his personal life and not his work—he was very close to losing his job. Management had given him a verbal warning. That's when he decided to call me.

Action Taken	
1	I facilitated an assessment of Tom's life. The first step was to understand his strengths, weaknesses and goals. Once I completed my fact-finding exercise, we reviewed the results and discussed a strategy to move forward.
2	Based on his goals, I established three priorities for Tom: career, health and the relationship with his wife.
3	I designed a strategy to help Tom accomplish his goals based on his three new priorities.

4	I developed a roadmap with daily milestones and a new routine to help Tom maintain structure.
5	I started developing his self-discipline skills using the five steps discussed throughout this book.
6	I created a strict routine (to be followed seven days a week). He texted me as soon as he woke up. His exercise routine started at five each morning before going to work—everything was closely monitored by me. I checked in with Tom at least three times a day (via text, email or phone). I would also call during his lunch break to ensure he was still very focused.
7	I trained his mind by treating every day equally.
8	I trained his mind to manage his emotions. I had him redirect negativity into positive energy and apply it towards his career.
9	I documented his progress in an Excel spreadsheet daily.
10	We had weekly (typically Saturday or Sunday) conversations to discuss progress and strategize on ways to continuously improve.
Results	
1	Negative situations just made him work harder now.
2	He consistently beat his job revenue targets.
3	Exercised five days a week.
4	Eventually he held himself accountable for his actions.

The Elderly Lady with Severe Arthritis

Sara was sixty-six, married and living in Seattle. She had severe arthritis and took heavy dosages of pain medicine just to get by every day. When she contacted me, she mentioned that she had never achieved her lifelong goals.

Sara ate too much junk food, was overweight, rarely exercised, and her range of motion was limited. Because of her physical pain level, it was very difficult for Sara to practice her musical instrument. She was running out of time and desperately needed guidance and someone to hold her accountable.

Action Taken	
1	I facilitated an assessment of Sara's life. The first step was to understand her strengths, weaknesses and goals. Once I completed my fact-finding exercise, we reviewed the results and discussed a strategy to move forward. After the evaluation we established one priority: health.
2	I started developing her self-discipline skills using the five steps discussed throughout this book to combat her health-related issues.

3	I established a roadmap with a new daily routine and health-related milestones such as eating healthier, exercising consistently and playing her musical instrument every day.
4	I trained her mind by mentoring her to treat every day equally. I had her follow the same routine seven days a week.
5	I began having her do strengthening work, aerobic exercises and stretching daily.
6	I had Sara email me the status of her activities daily. I would respond back and acknowledge her accomplishments. She thrived on positive feedback.
Results	
1	After fourteen months of mentoring, Sara has made remarkable progress in managing her arthritis and working toward her lifetime goals. She just hit the three-hour mark of practicing her instrument in one day.
2	She is doing extremely well with her program of aerobic exercise using an elliptical machine and recumbent bicycle.
3	She does Pilates twice a week and is now embarking on tai chi.
4	She has developed muscle tone, stamina and most important mental discipline to achieve her music and health-related goals. She actually has the discipline now to take anything on—but all within reason.
5	She holds herself accountable for her actions.

The Soon-To-Be-Ex-Executive

David was a very personable guy. He was married with three small children. He was the sole income earner in the family. He was a forty-four year-old marketing director who was about to get fired from his job. David had many challenges:

Poor leadership skills—always joking around, not respected by staff.

Poor self-discipline skills—disorganized, lacking focus, poor at goal management—prone to missing deadlines.

Unhealthy lifestyle—drank too much, overweight; prone to drinking too much, eating junk food, and never exercising.

David also did a horrible job trying to manage his finances. He spent like crazy and didn't even know how much until he could no longer keep up with his bills.

We needed to act quickly.

Action Taken	
1	I facilitated an assessment of David's life. The first step was to understand his strengths, weaknesses, goals, current routine, bad habits and activities. He had no self-discipline. Once I completed my fact-finding exercise, we reviewed the results and discussed a strategy to move forward.
2	We established two priorities: career and health.
3	I designed a strategy based on his two new priorities. This included adhering to the five steps to improve his self-discipline skills: 1. Instituting Structure 2. Prioritizing Your Life 3. Managing Time 4. Holding Yourself Accountable 5. Seeking Perfection The mentorship program evolved around these five areas as the catalyst for success.
4	I established a roadmap for David. It consisted of goals, milestones and a new daily routine.
5	I mentored David on how to be an effective leader. We focused on improving his communication skills, acting professional, nurturing key relationships and managing his staff effectively for maximum results.
6	I developed David's self-discipline skills daily by following the five steps discussed throughout this book.
7	I had David establish a to-do list every night. He emailed me a copy nightly and I held him accountable throughout the day.
8	I had David exercise every morning before he went to work.
9	I held David accountable daily via email, text and phone calls until I trained his mind so he can hold himself accountable.
10	I trained his mind to think with a sense of urgency. We repeated negative phrases that impacted him in a positive way.
11	We had weekly (typically Saturday or Sunday) conversations to discuss progress and strategize on ways to continuously improve.
Results	
1	David became more productive.
2	He managed time effectively.
3	He maintained structure throughout the day/evening.
4	David developed into an effective leader and within two years was promoted from a director to a vice president.
5	He consistently exercised six days a week.
6	He stopped drinking!
7	Eventually, his mind was trained to hold himself accountable for his actions.

Intelligent Yet Challenged

Robert was an intelligent, single and forty-two. He was extremely talented at writing and editing books, technically astute and great at building and fixing things with his hands. He was, however, horrible at managing his finances, cleaning his apartment, getting out of bed before noon. He was also overweight, wasted time, ate too much junk food, didn't exercise, and lacked focus. His mother actually called me to help her son.

Action Taken	
1	I facilitated an assessment of Robert's life. The first step was to understand his strengths, weaknesses and goals. Once I completed my fact-finding exercise, we reviewed the results and discussed a strategy to move forward.
2	Based on his goals, we established two priorities: career and health.
3	I designed a strategy based on his two new priorities. This included adhering to the five steps to improve his self-discipline skills: 1. Instituting Structure 2. Prioritizing Your Life 3. Managing Time 4. Holding Yourself Accountable 5. Seeking Perfection The mentorship program evolved around these five areas as the catalyst for success.
4	I developed a roadmap with goals, a daily routine and milestones to help Robert achieve his career and health related objectives. The goals were: eliminate sugar (he was addicted to the stuff), reduce junk food intake to once a week (he had been consuming it four times a week), reduce carbohydrate intake by half, and exercise a minimum of five days a week.
5	For his professional goals, we focused on how to improve managing his finances: creating and adhering to a budget, monitoring bank activity and opening a savings account.
6	I developed a business plan for his small business.
7	Created a to-do list nightly—he would also email me a copy.
8	He was accountable to me several times a day via email, text and phone calls until his mind was trained and he was able to hold himself accountable.
9	He maintained a daily log of all activities.
Results	
1	Robert lives by a budget.
2	His online business is growing nicely.
3	He's consistently exercising six days a week.
4	He eats properly.

5	Robert maintains a healthy weight.
6	He is effectively managing every aspect of his life.
7	His mind is now trained to hold himself accountable for his actions.

Tries to Take on the World and Shuts Down

Regina was a forty-six year-old single woman who worked in the hospitality industry. She came to me because she was disorganized, wasted time (severe procrastination) and spent countless hours dealing with family issues.

Regina had many goals and aspirations. She also had her fair share of daily obligations. There was so much going on in her life that on most days she became overwhelmed and would shut down and do nothing. That's when she decided to contact me.

Action Taken	
1	I facilitated an assessment of Regina's life. The first step was to understand her strengths, weaknesses and goals. Once I completed my fact-finding exercise, we reviewed the results and discussed a strategy to move forward.
2	Based on Regina's goals, I established two priorities for her: career and health.
3	I started developing her self-discipline skills using the five steps discussed throughout this book.
4	I developed a roadmap which included conservative and realistic milestones. We also documented a simple routine for her to follow seven days a week.
5	We placed several goals that weren't related to her two priorities on the back burner—we needed to keep her obligations, goals, tasks, projects manageable.
6	I had Regina establish a to-do list nightly. She would also email me a copy. I held her accountable to it throughout the day.
7	I provided her with detailed instructions on how to organize her email, apartment and office. I held her accountable daily to ensure she maintained structure.
8	I had her treat every day equally by following her new routine and adhere to her to-do list. Eventually her mind was trained to do so automatically.
9	I held her accountable to her to-do list several times a day (all seven days) via email, text and telephone calls.
10	I facilitated weekly (typically Saturday or Sunday) conversations to discuss progress and strategize on ways to continuously improve.
Results	

1	Regina is now organized and has more time to accomplish her daily milestones.
2	She no longer feels overwhelmed.
3	She consistently exercises.
4	She's extremely productive at work.
5	She designed and built a website for her new online business. She's been trying to develop and launch this site for three years.
6	She holds herself accountable for her actions

Small Business Owner with No Discipline

Ed was a thirty-eight year-old small business owner. He was married with two kids and lived in the Dallas area. He was making approximately $100,000 a year. When he contacted me he said "I should be making several million dollars a year—if I had some discipline in my life."

Ed was rarely motivated, unstructured, and wasted an extraordinary amount of time every day. He also lived an unhealthy lifestyle (he was overweight, ate too much junk food and didn't exercise).

Action Taken	
1	I facilitated an assessment of Ed's life. The first step was to understand his strengths, weaknesses and goals. Once I completed my fact-finding exercise, we reviewed my results and discussed a strategy to move forward.
2	Based on his goals, I determined that his two priorities should be career and health. He did a good job spending quality time with his family. That always gets top billing.
3	I started developing Ed's self-discipline skills based on the five steps discussed throughout this book.
4	I facilitated a one-day workshop to design a growth strategy for his business.
5	I developed a roadmap with goals, milestones and a daily routine for him to follow. We established some realistic health-related goals with conservative milestones initially.
6	I had Ed establish a to-do list every night (he emailed me a copy too). He needed to hit the ground running, focusing on his tasks, obligations and projects as soon as he woke up.
7	I had him organize his email and work environment at the end of each business day.
8	I mentored him to treat every day equally—focus was on his routine and to-do list first. Eventually it became habitual and his mind was trained.

9	I held him accountable to his to-do list several times a day via email, text and telephone calls until his mind was trained and he could hold himself accountable.
10	I facilitated weekly (typically Saturday or Sunday) conversations to discuss progress and strategize on ways to continuously improve.
Results	
1	Ed now has a thriving business with a staff of four people. Revenue is over one million dollars a year and growing.
2	He's consistently exercising a minimum of three days a week and reduced the amount of junk food he was consuming in half.
3	He trained his mind to hold himself accountable for his actions.

She Couldn't Study Consistently

Kim was a twenty-six year-old single woman. She had a good job, paying her about $65,000 a year. She owned a townhome in the San Francisco Bay area that her parents bought for her. She had a bachelor's degree in finance but wanted a master's degree as well.

She invested heavily to take her master's degree online. She failed miserably the first time around. She also paid a lot of money to take an advanced accounting course online, which would help her to eventually secure a higher-paying job. This was the third time she had paid for this finance course. She had failed previously because she couldn't motivate herself to study. One of her biggest problems was that she always wanted to hang out and party with her friends.

Action Taken	
1	I facilitated an assessment of Kim's life. The first step was to understand her strengths, weaknesses and goals. Once I completed my fact-finding exercise, we reviewed the results and discussed a strategy to move forward.
2	I established studying as the only priority in her life.
3	I started developing Kim's self-discipline skills to help her achieve her academic goals. The self-discipline mentoring was based on the five steps discussed throughout this book.
4	I developed a roadmap with realistic study-related milestones. The roadmap also included a new routine that would promote her study milestones. The routine included specific study times.
5	I had her establish a detailed to-do list nightly (included exact study hours and times)—she emailed me a copy every night.
6	I mentored her to focus on her routine and accomplishing her daily milestones. Nothing else mattered! Eventually her mind was trained and everything became habitual.

7	I mentored her to politely say no to hanging out with friends until her milestones were completed first each day.
8	She was accountable to me throughout the day and evening via telephone, text and email.
9	I had her send me a status nightly and logged the total study time into a spreadsheet—we would review her progress weekly. Our goal was to always beat her previous week's total study time—even if it was only by a few minutes.
Results	
1	Kim finally obtained her master's degree.
2	She completed her advanced course in finance.
3	She was recruited for a new job with a starting salary of **$80,000** a year.
4	Trained her mind to hold herself accountable for her actions.

The Entrepreneur

John wanted his own business. He was thirty-two and tired of working for someone else. He was always thinking of new ideas. Typically this is a good thing. However, rarely did one of John's ideas come to fruition. Occasionally when he did start on something, he was all over the board—absolutely no focus.

John was also very disorganized. Chaos was everywhere—his room, office, email, car. He was tired of being a failure; that's when he decided to call me.

Action Taken	
1	I facilitated an assessment of John's life. The first step was to understand his strengths, weaknesses and goals. Once I completed my fact-finding exercise, we reviewed the results and discussed a strategy to move forward.
2	We established career as his only priority.
3	I started developing John's self-discipline skills based on the five steps discussed throughout this book.
4	We documented and prioritized all of his current ideas.
5	We evaluated the top three ideas closely, strategizing, discussing competition and brainstorming the challenges with each—eventually picked one.
6	We developed a business plan for his new venture.
7	I established a daily routine based on his career. I ensured that John focused on his daily routine and milestones first each day.
8	I had John establish a to-do list nightly and made sure he adhered to it throughout the day.

9	Every time John had a new idea it was emailed to me. I would save it on my computer: we discussed his ideas once a week. I kept him very focused on his current project.
10	He was accountable to me several times a day via email, text and telephone calls.
11	I facilitated weekly (typically Saturday or Sunday) conversations to discuss progress and strategize on ways to continuously improve.
Results	
1	John built a successful Web-based business.
2	He developed self-discipline skills (excelled in time and goal management).
3	He remained focused on his daily milestones.
4	He was accountable to himself for his actions.

The Overweight and Disorganized Business Owner

Ben was a single, thirty-five year-old businessman. He was a workaholic and loved it. His business was growing at a good pace, however, he felt that it could grow much faster.

When he first contacted me Ben was fifty-five pounds overweight and had no motivation to improve his unhealthy lifestyle. He didn't exercise, ate too much junk food, smoked, and drank heavily. He was also very disorganized—he had no structure in his life. He needed some guidance and direction.

Action Taken	
1	I facilitated an assessment of Ben's life (e.g., strengths, challenges, goals, daily routine). Once I completed my fact-finding exercise, we reviewed the results and discussed a strategy to move forward.
2	We set health as his priority—but as an extension of his professional life. Ben's world revolved around business. With Ben it was the only way—he was consumed with work all day. I convinced him that exercise should be part of his career—the healthier he became, the more energy and stamina he would have for his business.
3	I started developing Ben's self-discipline skills based on the five steps discussed throughout this book.
4	I developed a roadmap with goals, milestones and a daily routine.
5	I had Ben establish a to-do list nightly and held him accountable to it throughout the day.
6	I held Ben accountable to his new daily routine that promoted a healthier lifestyle, while keeping him focused on his career.
7	I mentored him on how to organize his office space, categorized and prioritized his huge to-do list and setup all of his appointments in MS Outlook.

8	We reviewed Ben's food and caloric intake daily. It was managed closely.
9	He was accountable to me at least twice a day via telephone, text and email (seven days a week). I wanted to make sure that he was focused on his routine and milestones first every day. I also wanted to make sure that he followed his to-do list.
10	I facilitated weekly (typically Saturday or Sunday) conversations to discuss progress and strategize on ways to continuously improve.
Results	
1	Ben lost all of his weight and manages his eating habits daily to make sure it stays off.
2	He only drinks socially now.
3	He has stamina—more energetic.
4	He accomplishes more because he remains organized—his mind is no longer seeing clutter everywhere—he no longer wastes time looking for things.
5	He consistently exercises. He used to leave his house by seven each morning; now he leaves at and goes to the gym to work out for thirty minutes, takes a shower and is still at work by seven-thirty.
6	He holds himself accountable for his actions.

The High-Rolling Senior Executive

Terrance was a thirty-seven-year-old senior vice president making $300,000 a year. He's married with two young children. You might say that Terrance was doing extremely well. So why did he contact me?

Terrance was in severe debt, didn't know how much he spent each day/week/month, lived well beyond his means (extremely lavish lifestyle) and had all of his eggs in one basket (one employer).

He had very little to his name: his home was rented, credit cards were maxed out and his fancy car was leased. If he was laid off tomorrow, he would be homeless; he had no savings. He had no discipline: he managed time poorly and couldn't exercise consistently.

Action Taken	
1	I facilitated an assessment of Terrance's life. The first step was to understand his strengths, weaknesses and goals. Once I completed my fact-finding exercise, we reviewed the results and discussed a strategy to move forward.
2	I reviewed all of his bank's financial data in detail for over a two months.

3	I set career, finances and health as priorities. He already did a good job spending quality time with his family.
4	I started developing Terrance's self-discipline skills based on the five steps discussed throughout this book.
5	I developed a roadmap with goals, milestones, a daily routine and a process to monitor and ensure accountability.
6	We established a budget so Terrance could manage his finances, with my oversight. I insisted that I have full access to his bank accounts to monitor activity daily.
7	I had Terrance open a savings account.
8	I held Terrance accountable several times a day to his routine and milestones via phone calls, text and email.
9	I facilitated weekly (typically Saturday or Sunday) conversations to discuss progress and strategize on ways to continuously improve.
Results	
1	Terrance exercises every morning at six before going to work.
2	He has eliminated his credit card debt.
3	His expenditures have been reduced by 60 percent.
4	He has a savings account with a modest balance.
5	He improved his leadership and self-discipline skills.
6	He is more productive throughout the day.
7	He holds himself accountable for his actions.

BUILDING COMPETITIVE ORGANIZATIONS

Do the same principles I've outlined in this book apply to help organizations become more efficient? Yes and no. Yes, every organization needs to institute *structure, prioritize* their projects and manage *time* efficiently, while employees need to hold themselves *accountable* and *seek perfection*. However, there are several additional steps required to ensure a successful transformation. Below I've highlighted the three-step process to build a competitive organization.

The 3-Step Process

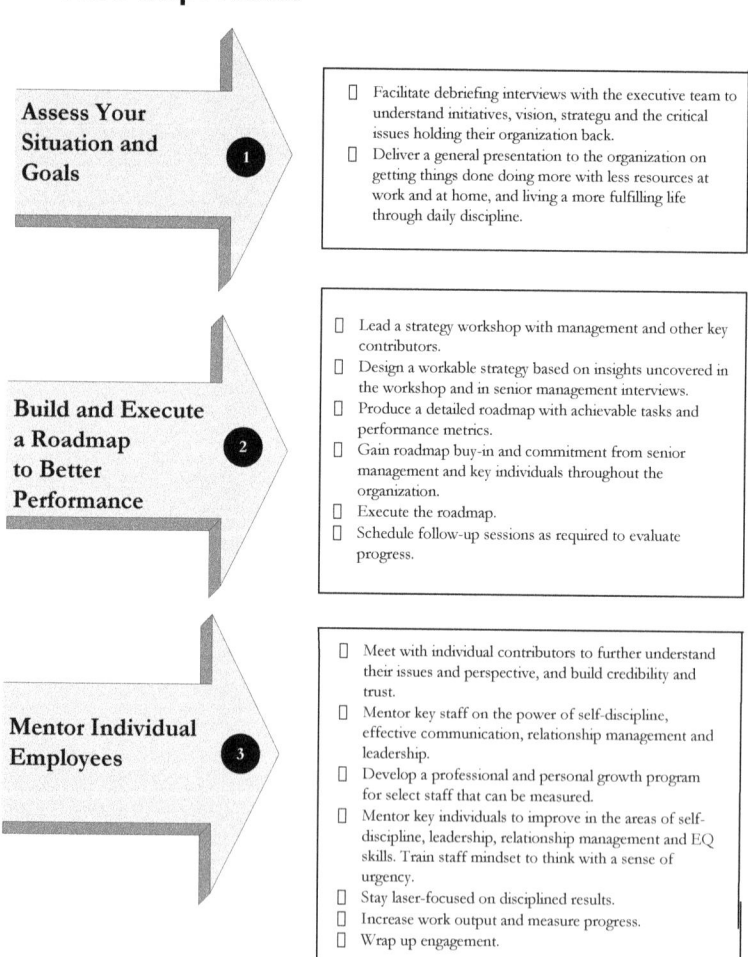

Assess Your Situation and Goals — 1
- Facilitate debriefing interviews with the executive team to understand initiatives, vision, strategu and the critical issues holding their organization back.
- Deliver a general presentation to the organization on getting things done doing more with less resources at work and at home, and living a more fulfilling life through daily discipline.

Build and Execute a Roadmap to Better Performance — 2
- Lead a strategy workshop with management and other key contributors.
- Design a workable strategy based on insights uncovered in the workshop and in senior management interviews.
- Produce a detailed roadmap with achievable tasks and performance metrics.
- Gain roadmap buy-in and commitment from senior management and key individuals throughout the organization.
- Execute the roadmap.
- Schedule follow-up sessions as required to evaluate progress.

Mentor Individual Employees — 3
- Meet with individual contributors to further understand their issues and perspective, and build credibility and trust.
- Mentor key staff on the power of self-discipline, effective communication, relationship management and leadership.
- Develop a professional and personal growth program for select staff that can be measured.
- Mentor key individuals to improve in the areas of self-discipline, leadership, relationship management and EQ skills. Train staff mindset to think with a sense of urgency.
- Stay laser-focused on disciplined results.
- Increase work output and measure progress.
- Wrap up engagement.

Step 1: Assess Your Situation and Goals

Acquire an understanding of the organization's culture, issues, political atmosphere, business challenges and initiatives. Once you're familiar with the landscape, facilitate an interactive presentation on how to build a world-class organization.

You are trying to introduce change into an organization. Your presentation should answer two questions: How to build a world-class organization and how to improve the quality of life for everyone? Showcase the following:

❑ **Discipline:** A staff that is disciplined possesses a sense of urgency, has excellent time management skills and is always focused on their goals. There are no boundaries when the organization is disciplined. With discipline comes efficiency. The more efficient you are at work, the more personal time you will have to enjoy at home.

❑ **Having a better quality of life:** Organizational efficiency doesn't start and end with discipline. It's also important to manage professional relationships, communicate effectively and develop good leadership skills. The most effective way to get everyone's attention is to ensure the changes you are introducing will result in a better quality of life for everyone. That means a reasonable work week of forty to fifty hours.

❑ **Instill structure for efficiency:**
   • **Implement streamlined processes.** Organizations often have few or no processes or there are too many and they are very burcaucratic. The more streamlined the processes, the more efficient the organization.
   • **Maintain organized work environments.** The more organized the environment, the more productive the organization. The more organized the individual, the more productive the individual.

The objectives of this step are to gain credibility from your audience and to paint a positive vision for adopting discipline.

Step 2: Build and Execute a Roadmap to Better Performance

Facilitate a strategy workshop to assist your organization to quickly address people, process and performance challenges through a comprehensive three-day process. The overall objectives of the workshop should be to identify specific issues and develop a roadmap that has the *buy-in, commitment,* and *ownership* of key representatives of the organization. The workshop should produce the following outcomes:

- ❏ A collective agreement and buy-in of the people, process and performance issues facing your organization.
- ❏ Categorization and prioritization of issues.
- ❏ Identification of root causes of the current problems.
- ❏ An intelligent plan of action (roadmap) based on the facts of your current environment.
- ❏ Buy-in, commitment, and ownership of the roadmap throughout the organization, bottom up and top down.

Strategy Workshop Agenda

The workshop should be comprised of three days of off-site, structured, facilitated exercises, which focuses on the business challenges first, and also the people, process and performance issues. Different key members of your organization participate at different times, typically divided into three sessions: *key management, non-management representatives,* and a *joint planning session.* Several customers who use the organization's services can also participate.

The joint planning session includes representatives from both management and non-management, who work together to integrate the plans developed during the previous sessions into a single, cohesive roadmap, which is presented to the executive sponsoring the workshop. The table below highlights the three-day agenda.

Day One (Management Team)	Day Two (Non-Management Team)	Day Three (Joint Session: Mgmt. & Non-Mgmt.)
Introduction. Communicate the process and the objectives of the workshop.	Introduction, day 1 review.	Overview of day 1 & day 2.
Identify detailed business issues, initiatives and drivers.	Identify people, process and performance issues.	Representatives from both management and non-management staff work together to integrate the plans developed during the previous sessions into a single, cohesive action plan.
Identify people, process and performance issues.	Work with the group to organize and prioritize issues.	Formalize action plan into presentation.
Discuss and brainstorm issues and potential solutions.	Design a "straw man" strategy and action plan to address top issues.	Present to executive management the final action plan (roadmap).
Organize, categorize and prioritize the top 3-5 brainstormed issues into an action plan.	Present a "straw man" action plan to management team from day 1.	Get buy-in and commitment from the entire organization in order to move forward with one roadmap.
Design "straw man" strategy and action plan to address top issues.	Management presents their findings to non-management team.	Summarize and discuss next steps.
Summarize and discuss next steps.	Summarize and discuss next steps.	

Workshop Objectives

The session objectives are to:

❏ Present an overview of commonly-occurring organizational issues.

❏ Identify detailed business issues, initiatives and drivers.

❏ Identify organizational issues such as poor communication and too much bureaucracy.

❏ Identify details of the current organization, its history and its evolution.

❏ Discuss and brainstorm issues and potential solution

strategies.
- ❏ Organize, categorize and prioritize the brainstormed issues into a roadmap.

Workshop Deliverables
Workshop deliverables include:
- ❏ Structured, facilitated workshop.
- ❏ Top organizational issues, opportunities for improvement and recommended solutions.
- ❏ A roadmap developed by the workshop participants with tasks identified and accountability assigned.
- ❏ Across-the-board buy-in of the roadmap.

Who Should Attend
The strategy workshop is ideal for:
- ❏ Senior managers, mid-level managers and executives looking to improve customer satisfaction, employee productivity and reduce risk.
- ❏ Key staff interested in improving their ability to support and manage the environment.
- ❏ Key customers of your organization.

The workshop will take a total of three days onsite. The 3rd day of the workshop is designated for finalizing the roadmap with the executive sponsor.

Step 3: Mentor Individual Employees
A leader's top priority is to build the right team to implement strategies. The objective is to develop average employees into superstars to implement a roadmap in a timely manner. The most effective way to achieve this is to facilitate one-on-one mentoring to help develop non-technical skills such as self-discipline, leadership, relationship management.

Build the Right Team
The first step to build an efficient and highly productive staff is to determine the caliber of talent in your organization. Success is based primarily on the shoulders of your most talented employees. Let's say you have an organization of twenty people. The mixture of

superior, above-average and average employees could look like this:
- ❏ Superior Employees = 10 percent
- ❏ Above-Average Employees = 30 percent
- ❏ Average Employees = 60 percent

Ideally the mixture for success should be:
- ❏ Superior Employees = 40 percent
- ❏ Above-Average Employees = 40 percent
- ❏ Average Employees = 20 percent

SUPERIOR	ABOVE-AVERAGE	AVERAGE
Motivated (24-7-365)	Motivated	Occasionally needs to be motivated
Completes tasks on schedule and most of the time ahead of schedule	Completes tasks on schedule	Typically requires guidance
Intelligent	Intelligent	Poor time management skills
Extremely productive. Priorities are career, health and relationship management. (Typically works after normal workday is complete.)	Productive	Lacks focus
Creative (can think out of the box)	Creative	Not goal-oriented
Focused	Focused	Not a leader
Extremely dependable	Dependable	
Manages time and energy efficiently	Good time management	
Very goal-oriented	Good goal management	
Very resourceful	Resourceful	
Excellent communication skills	Good communication skills	
Excellent leadership skills	Good leadership skills	
Thinks with a sense of urgency		
Very confident		
Controls emotions—can redirect negative emotions into career		
Exercises consistently		

You would like more *superior employees*—who wouldn't? Perform a thorough assessment of key staff to determine their capability. See Appendix C for the actual questionnaire used during an assessment for individual contributors and Appendix D for a questionnaire used to evaluate management.

One-on-One Mentoring

Once the assessment has been completed, design a strategy and a roadmap for individuals to develop their skills. The roadmap should include goals, priorities, milestones, a new routine, and accountability metrics. The roadmap is used as the catalyst for one-on-one mentoring. Invest in your staff. For more details about one-on-one mentoring, visit www.disciplinementor.com.

ORGANIZATION CASE STUDIES

I learned early in my career that undisciplined people congregate in undisciplined organizations. Whether I dealt with a fast-paced financial services company, or a very slow bureaucratic and highly political government agency, they all shared similar people challenges, such as:

- ❏ Poor time management
- ❏ Lack of focus
- ❏ Poor to average leadership skills
- ❏ No sense of urgency
- ❏ Poor communication
- ❏ Severe procrastination
- ❏ Lack of structure
- ❏ Poor goal management techniques

These issues were universal regardless of the business model, corporate initiatives, vision, strategy and goals. Below are actual case studies I facilitated in Fortune 500 and Global 2000 companies. The approaches to resolving the issues were almost identical, whether the company was incorporated or family-owned, headquartered in the United States or Asia.

	Transportation Company, Hong Kong
OVERVIEW	They were a monopoly in the transportation industry, a very profitable, multi-billion dollar corporation. Phrases like great customer service, highly efficient and high productivity were not synonymous with this company. It performed poorly on all fronts (e.g., customer service, sales). However, it didn't matter how the company executed because it was always profitable. Suddenly there were new companies cropping up everywhere, and for the first time in its history the company had serious competitors. I was brought in to promote change and institute discipline.
CHALLENGES	✔ Organizational resistance to change ✔ Departmental inefficiency (lack of processes) ✔ Poor communication throughout the company ✔ Ineffective leadership ✔ No sense of urgency ✔ Expenditures were too high
ACTION STEPS	1. Met with executive management to understand business goals, vision, strategy, initiatives and organization challenges from their perspective. 2. Facilitated corporate-wide presentations (sponsored by HR and the CEO) on how to build great organizations and improve their quality of life. The presentations also included the topics of change, instituting structure and a customer service-oriented mentality throughout the company. 3. Facilitated detailed assessments of key departments (e.g., customer service, sales and IT). 4. Facilitated workshops to design a new companywide strategy, and develop a roadmap to address the top people, process and performance issues. 5. Assisted in the execution of the roadmap. 6. In conjunction with HR, developed and executed a professional growth program (PGP) for key staff and management. The PGP highlighted each person's strengths, weaknesses and goals. It also included individual roadmaps with specific milestones. The PGP was different than the traditional (passive) HR-sponsored performance reviews. It was an active process that is the catalyst to monitor and drive employee performance throughout the year. 7. Facilitated one-on-one mentoring to address weaknesses and develop key skills such as self-discipline and leadership. 8. Using output from the workshops, helped design new organization structures to better meet the demands of the business. 9. Provided guidance on designing and implementing streamlined processes. 10. Facilitated quarterly mini-workshops (checkups) to review roadmap progress and address any new issues as they arose. 11. Mentored individuals on how to stay focused and work with a sense of urgency.
RESULTS	✔ Customer service improved dramatically. ✔ Teamwork and communication improved. ✔ Instilled a sense of urgency. ✔ Improved performance of several key individuals.

Media Company, Atlanta

OVERVIEW

The company was growing at an exponential pace. It always focused on technology. Very little effort was spent on people, process and performance issues. Employees were frustrated.

The corporate strategy was to purchase smaller companies that complemented their suite of services. Once purchased, these companies needed to be integrated.

The new executive management team wanted results quickly They turned to IT to implement a new technology strategy with very aggressive deadlines. Unfortunately, IT wasn't effective. It already had an overabundance of people, process and technology issues to deal with.

CHALLENGES

- Unstable production environment.
- Lack of structure (e.g. critical processes).
- Staff was always in a reactive mode.
- Poor communication between departments.
- Lack of leadership skills throughout the organization.
- Lack of teamwork.
- Frustration and burnout proliferated throughout the organization.
- Although engineering and IT operations were under the same organization, they weren't working as one unit.

ACTION STEPS

1. Facilitated a presentation to the IT organization on how to build the ideal environment which, will also improve their quality of life. Some of the topics included how to:
   a. Manage key relationships
   b. Effectively say no
   c. Improve communication
   d. Institute and maintain structure
   e. Improve overall productivity by developing self-discipline skills (time management, goal management)

2. Facilitated an organization assessment to determine most critical people, process and performance issues.
3. Facilitated a workshop to design a strategy to integrate newly acquired businesses and develop a roadmap to resolve the top issues.
4. Implemented a Professional Growth Program (PGP) for key individual contributors and management. The PGP was used to develop key skills (e.g., self-discipline, leadership). Upon completion, it was used as the catalyst for one-on-one coaching sessions.
5. Facilitated one-on-one discipline-mentoring for staff and management to improve efficiency.
6. Determined key organization success factors.
7. Determined current baseline productivity numbers (KPIs).
8. Determined new KPIs for success.
9. Developed leadership skills of key individual contributors and management.
10. Mentored staff on how to continuously strategize.
11. Mentored organizational staff members on how to hold themselves accountable for their actions by training their minds.
12. Implemented several critical infrastructure support processes. (Charge Management, Problem Management and Production Acceptance).

RESULTS

✔ Improved leadership skills for key individuals.
✔ Improved reliability and availability of technical infrastructure.
✔ Improved teamwork and communication.
✔ Improved service delivery to customers.
✔ Improved performance of key staff.
✔ Instilled a sense of urgency throughout the organization.
✔ Customer Satisfaction improved.

Entertainment Company, Los Angeles

OVERVIEW

Executive management designed an aggressive three-year strategy. Unfortunately, management knew it couldn't move the organization quickly enough to meet their deadlines.

Employees had a difficult time embracing change. A big success factor was how quickly the IT organization could help implement the technology for the new strategy; unfortunately, they weren't very effective. The technology was the easy part. The people problems were enormous.

CHALLENGES

✔ An IT organization not structured properly to address the needs of the business. It actually had two separate internal technical support departments:
✔ Highly political atmosphere.
✔ Poor communication between departments.
✔ Bureaucratic environment—ineffective processes.
✔ Duplication of efforts in some areas.
✔ No sense of urgency.
✔ Poor time management.

ACTION STEPS

1. Presented to staff on how to build a world-class organization. The objective was to build the ideal environment (efficient, cost-effective and disciplined) to improve everyone's quality of life. Other topics included, how to:
   a. Improve overall productivity by adopting discipline and developing self-discipline skills (time management, goal management).
   b. Manage key relationships.
   c. Improve communication.
   d. Prioritize and stay focused.
   e. Maintain structure.
   f. Self-motivation.

2. Completed an assessment to determine most critical issues.
3. Facilitated a workshop to design a strategy to align with business objectives and develop a roadmap to address the top people, process and performance issues.
4. Implemented a Professional Growth Program (PGP) for individual contributors and management. The PGP was used as the vehicle to develop key skills (e.g., self-discipline, leadership). Upon completion, the PGP was used as the catalyst for one-on-one coaching sessions.
5. Facilitated one-on-one mentoring of several key staff to develop crucial skills, including self-discipline, leadership, communication.
6. Determined success factors to build a world class organization.
7. Determined current KPIs.
8. Determined new baseline productivity KPIs.
9. Implemented a new organization structure with one technical support team.

RESULTS

- ✔ Removed organization barriers and improved teamwork.
- ✔ Eliminated bureaucracy.
- ✔ Improved overall productivity by fifteen percent.
- ✔ Improved performance of several key staff.
- ✔ Instilled a sense of urgency throughout the organization.
- ✔ Improved leadership skills of several key staff.
- ✔ Improved communication throughout the organization.

Entertainment Company, New Zealand

OVERVIEW

The CEO wanted to integrate the Broadcast Engineering Department with Information Technology (IT).

IT was a very cost-effective and efficient department. Over the years they invested in industry best practices equally in the three primary areas: people, processes and technology.

Engineering had good technology but lacked streamlined processes. The staff was also set in their ways—introducing change wasn't going to be easy. The average tenure for an engineer was twenty-five years.

CHALLENGES

- ✔ Poor communication between Engineering and IT.
- ✔ Highly political environment.
- ✔ Engineers were resistant to change.

ACTION STEPS

1. Presented to IT and Engineering staff on how to build a world-class organization based on industry best practices focusing on people, process and performance.
2. Completed an assessment to determine most critical issues for both organizations.
3. Facilitated a workshop to design a strategy to integrate both organizations and develop a roadmap to address the top people, process and performance issues.
4. Held organizations accountable to the tasks outlined in the roadmap.
5. Implemented a Professional Growth Program (PGP) for key staff. The PGP was used to develop key self-discipline skills. Upon completion, the PGP was used as the catalyst for one-on-one coaching sessions.
6. Facilitated one-on-one mentoring for key staff and management to adopt change and develop their self-discipline skills.
7. Facilitated a two-hour workshop to design a new organization structure.
8. Assisted in the redesign of a Problem Management process to be used to resolve all technical issues throughout the company.

RESULTS

- ✔ Improved communication.
- ✔ Improved leadership skills for several key managers.
- ✔ Restructured the organization and established one Technical Support organization.
- ✔ Improved customer service.
- ✔ Eliminated duplicate functions which saved the company money.

Recruitment Company, Los Angeles

OVERVIEW

The president of the company wanted to increase revenue by fifty percent. It was certainly doable with the right team.

He had thirteen recruiters, but only one was a superstar. All recruiters were paid solely on commission. You would think that anyone who was getting paid by commission only would do whatever it takes to make their quota—nope.

CHALLENGES

✔ Most of the recruiters had poor time management skills
✔ No sense of urgency. They actually had a nine-to-five mentality
✔ Lack of focus
✔ Unstructured
✔ Disorganized environment
✔ Didn't follow an efficient routine
✔ Not all followed a to-do list

ACTION STEPS

1. Presented to staff on how to be more productive by developing their self-discipline skills.
2. Facilitated a workshop to design a strategy to dramatically increase sales and develop a roadmap to address the top issues.
3. Worked with management to implement tasks outlined in the roadmap.
4. Facilitated an evaluation of every recruiter.
5. Implemented a Professional Growth Program (PGP) for individual contributors and management. The PGP was used to develop key skills (e.g., self-discipline, sense of urgency, leadership). Upon completion, the PGP was used as the catalyst for one-on-one mentoring sessions.
6. Mentored key staff to develop their self-discipline skills. Did not mentor everyone—some individuals were not worth the investment. It was unfortunate but they were fired by the president.

RESULTS

✔ Improved overall productivity (sales calls, marketing efforts, etc.) by forty percent.
✔ Revenue increased by thirty percent.
✔ Individuals improved their time management skills.
✔ Instilled a sense of urgency mentality throughout the organization.
✔ Instituted structure throughout the organization to improve efficiency.

Technology Company, Philadelphia

OVERVIEW	New senior vice president of IT wanted to implement a new strategy quickly to help meet the demands of the business. Unfortunately, the organization culture was very laid back, like a union shop. They did the bare minimum to squeak by every day. There was no urgency to make quick improvements. Change was not going to be easy.

CHALLENGES	✔ The organization lacked discipline
	  • Poor time and goal management.
	  • Lack of focus.
	✔ Employees did the bare minimum
	  • Company culture was not to layoff anyone. Very difficult to raise the productivity level with this type of culture.
	✔ Poor communication throughout the organization.
	✔ No new headcount was budgeted for the organization even though the company kept growing—the demands kept increasing.

ACTION STEPS	1. Presented to staff on how to build a world-class organization. The topics included, how to:
	  a. Improve overall productivity by adopting discipline.
	  b. Manage key relationships.
	  c. Improve communication.
	  d. Improve your quality of life.
	  e. Instill a sense of urgency.
	  f. How to say no effectively.
	2. Facilitated a workshop to design a strategy which, aligns with business growth and develop a roadmap to address the top people, process and performance issues. The workshop participants included key staff and management.
	3. Evaluated key staff to better understand its strengths and weaknesses.
	4. Implemented a Professional Growth Program (PGP) for individual contributors and management. The PGP was used to develop key skills. Upon completion, the PGP was used as the catalyst for one-on-one coaching sessions.
	5. Facilitated one-on-one discipline mentoring for key staff to help them become more productive, hold themselves accountable and instill a sense of urgency.
	6. Determined success factors.
	7. Determined current baseline numbers (KPIs).
	8. Determined new baseline productivity numbers (KPIs).
	9. Rated success factors monthly to determine progress or lack thereof.

RESULTS	✔ Improved organization productivity. ✔ Improved performance of several key staff. ✔ Improved leadership skills of several key staff. ✔ Improved communication. ✔ The laid-back mentality disappeared. There was now a sense of urgency. ✔ Implemented the new roadmap.

State Government, Australia	
OVERVIEW	IT support functions were decentralized throughout the government. Each agency had their own IT organization—doing their own thing. There was a big government initiative agency-wide, to reduce costs. The new CIO needed to centralize all IT functions to eliminate duplication of efforts.
CHALLENGES	✔ Highly political environment. ✔ Staff lacked a sense of urgency—had a laid back nine-to-five government-union employee type of demeanor. ✔ Highly bureaucratic environment. ✔ Difficult to introduce change. ✔ Poor communication between agencies. ✔ Perception that current centralized IT organization was not responsive to agencies.

ACTION STEPS	1. Presented to staff on how to build a world-class organization. Topics discussed included, how to:
	  a. Improve overall productivity by adopting discipline.
	  b. Manage key relationships.
	  c. Improve communication.
	  d. Improve your quality of life.
	2. Facilitated a workshop to design a strategy to integrate IT functions and develop a roadmap to address the top people, process and performance issues. One of the workshop's objectives was to get buy-in throughout the organization to centralize IT functions.
	3. Facilitated evaluations for key individual contributors and management.
	4. Implemented a Professional Growth Program (PGP) for individual contributors and management. The PGP was used to develop key self-discipline, sense of urgency, leadership. Upon completion, the PGP was used as the catalyst for one-on-one mentoring sessions.
	5. Mentored key staff and management on how to develop self-discipline skills and to embrace change.

RESULTS	✔ Centralized IT function. ✔ Improved performance and leadership skills of several key staff. ✔ Improved communication. ✔ Reduced bureaucracy for IT support. ✔ Reduced operating costs.

County Government, South Florida

OVERVEW	The CIO wanted to move forward with a highly visible, politically-motivated, county-wide initiative. Unfortunately, his staff wasn't thrilled about changing the current mode of operation. Staffers had cushy government jobs. They worked from nine to five and not a minute more.
CHALLENGES	✔ Highly political environment. ✔ Lack of urgency among staff. ✔ Unmotivated staff—just there to pick up a paycheck. They worked the bare minimum and showed no initiative. ✔ Weak management team. ✔ Poor communication. ✔ Too much bureaucracy.

ACTION STEPS	1. Presented to staff on how to build a world-class organization. The objective was to get buy-in and commitment to move forward with one strategy. The topics included, how to:
	  a. Improve overall productivity.
	  b. Manage key relationships.
	  c. Improve communication.
	  d. Improve your quality of life.
	  e. Accomplish more in less time.
	  f. Prioritize and say no effectively.
	
	2. Facilitated a workshop to design a strategy for the new county-wide initiative and develop a roadmap to address the top people, process and performance challenges.
	3. Facilitated evaluations of individual contributors and management.
	4. Implemented a Professional Growth Program (PGP) for individual contributors and management. The PGP was used to develop key skills. Upon completion, the PGP was used as the catalyst for one-on-one mentoring sessions.
	5. Facilitated one-on-one mentoring for staff and management.
	6. Held the team accountable to the tasks outlined in the roadmap. Also trained their minds on how to hold themselves accountable.
	7. Helped design streamlined processes.
	8. Determined success factors.
	9. Determined current baseline productivity numbers.
	10. Determined new baseline productivity numbers for success.
	11. Monitored and rated success factors consistently.

RESULTS	✔ Improved communication throughout the organization. ✔ Saw staff complete major projects on schedule and under budget. ✔ Improved overall morale. ✔ Staff was more efficient at work and at home. Several average and above-average-rated employees developed into superstars. ✔ Instilled a sense of urgency in the organization. ✔ Improved overall performance by 20 percent.

	Large Financial Services Company, New York City
OVERVEW	The business had a very negative impression of IT, and rightly so. Overall support and development of technology was poor. IT was never an enabler for the business. They were looked upon as overhead. The company hired a new CIO to turn things around quickly.
CHALLENGES	✔ Poor customer service. ✔ Staff mainly in a reactive mode. ✔ Lack of leaders. ✔ Poor communication. ✔ Lack of streamlined processes. ✔ Failure to follow industry best practices. ✔ Poor cost-effectiveness. ✔ Unmotivated team. ✔ Poor RAS (Reliability, Availability, Serviceability) throughout the infrastructure

ACTION STEPS	1. Presented to staff on how to build a world-class organization. The topics included, how to:
	  a. Improve your quality of life.
	  b. Implement industry best practices.
	  c. Improve communication.
	  d. Prioritize and focus.
	  e. Work with urgency.
	  f. Institute structure for efficiency.
	
	2. Facilitated a workshop to design a strategy to improve IT's stature in the business and develop a roadmap to address the top people, process and performance issues.
	3. Facilitated individual assessments for key staff.
	4. Implemented a Professional Growth Program (PGP) for individual contributors and management. The PGP was used to develop key skills. Upon completion, the PGP was used as the catalyst for one-on-one coaching sessions to improve individual performance.
	5. Facilitated one-on-one mentoring for key staff to improve leadership, self-discipline, and communication skills.
	6. Determined organization success factors.
	7. Determined current baseline productivity numbers.
	8. Determined new baseline productivity numbers.
	9. Provided guidance to design streamlined processes.
	10. Established a new Personal Productivity Services function located within the business with its sole charter to help their analysts be more productive with their desktop computing infrastructure.
	11. Helped organization institute structure:
	  a. Organized individual work areas (desks, files, email).
	  b. Established efficient routines.
	  c. Everyone was required to follow a to-do list every day.

RESULTS	✔ Improved service delivery throughout the enterprise (customer satisfaction improved dramatically). ✔ Improved teamwork and communication. ✔ Improved performance of key staff. ✔ Instilled a sense of urgency throughout the organization. ✔ Got organization recognized as a business enabler—no longer a hindrance.

IT Service Provider, North Carolina

OVERVEW

CEO of the company had very aggressive sales goals. He wanted to increase revenue by 25 percent ASAP.

CHALLENGES

✔ Sales team weren't working very efficiently.
✔ Ineffective leadership.
✔ Poor time management throughout the organization.
✔ Organizational lack of structure.
✔ Disorganized individuals.
✔ No sense of urgency.

ACTION STEPS

1. Presented to staff on how to build a world-class organization. The topics included how to:
   a. Improve your quality of life.
   b. Manage relationships.
   c. Improve communication.
   d. Work with urgency.
   e. Institute structure for efficiency.

2. Facilitated a workshop to design a strategy to increase sales and develop a roadmap to address the top people, process and performance issues.
3. Facilitated individual assessments for the entire Sales Team.
4. Implemented a Professional Growth Program (PGP) for individual contributors and management. The PGP was used to develop key skills. Upon completion, the PGP was used as the catalyst for one-on-one coaching sessions to improve individual performance.
5. Mentored team to develop self-discipline skills. This included how to hold themselves accountable for their actions.
6. Determined success factors.
7. Determined current baseline productivity numbers.
8. Determined new baseline productivity numbers.
9. Instituted structure throughout the organization.
10. Provided guidance to design streamlined processes.
11. Helped organization instill structure:
    a. Organized individual work areas.
    b. Established efficient routines.
    c. Required everyone to follow a to-do list every day.

RESULTS

✔ Increased company revenues by fifteen percent in the first year with the same head count.
✔ Made sales team more efficient in their job—even when it came to administrative tasks.
✔ Instilled a sense of urgency throughout the organization.
✔ Improved leadership skills of several key staff.
✔ Improved communication.

EPILOGUE

The Legacy

"You begin saving the world by saving one person at a time; all
else is grandiose romanticism or politics."
Charles Bukowski

What else could I possibly want out of life? Why can't I just kick
back and take it easy? I've done it all. I've accomplished every goal
both personal and professional. So enough is enough, right? What
could possibly top the success I have already achieved? The answer
is quite simple: *Discipline*. I've been saying it to my friends for
decades but didn't realize the impact of it until I was in my forties.

If I cross the street tomorrow and get run over by a truck, it's
not enough that the people I've mentored to be disciplined will
have something for the rest of their lives to remember me by. It's
not enough that I've made them productive or that I've helped them
to help themselves become successful. It's not enough that I've
written many books, exercised consistently all my adult life, and
had a successful career. *I want more!* I want to have a major impact
on people that I've never met before. I want to be remembered by
one word and that's *discipline*. Many people need guidance to make
the most out of their existence. I want them to turn to discipline
now, and even when I'm long gone.

Right now the word *discipline* is rarely used at home or at the
office. The most common place you hear it is when professional
athletes are in rigorous training or occasionally at the gym amongst
some hardcore bodybuilders. Mentioned elsewhere, it is usually in
the context of punitive discipline. Discipline should not be viewed
as punishment, or couched as something negative. Mentoring on
the importance of discipline is the best gift a parent can give to
their son or daughter. My ultimate goal is to leave that legacy for
adults. Life is no longer about just completing goals. Bernard Shaw
says it best:

"This is the true joy in life, the being recognized by yourself as
a mighty one; the being thoroughly worn out before you are thrown
on the scrap heap; the being a force of nature instead of a feverish

selfish little clod of ailments and grievances complaining that the world will not devote itself to making you happy.

I am of the opinion that my life belongs to the whole community and as long as I live it is my privilege to do for whatever I can. I want to be thoroughly used up when I die for the harder I work the more I live. I rejoice in life for its own sake. Life is no brief candle to me. It is a sort of splendid torch which I have got hold of for the moment, and I want to make it burn as brightly as possible before handing it on to future generations."

Do it for the Children

Parents want the very best for their kids. There is no greater gift that you can pass on to your kids then helping them to become disciplined. It's rewarding to see their faces light up when they apply discipline for themselves and realize its impact. Second, your life will be infinitely easier if you've instilled in your children discipline from the start because everyone will be happier and well-adjusted. Third, you need to do it for society. What do you want to contribute to society? A happy, well-adjusted child or one who struggles at every turn?

If you are not disciplined yourself, don't expect your kids to be. It doesn't mean that every disciplined parent will end up with a disciplined child. Each individual is built differently. But they all should be taught this ongoing lesson at every opportunity. Don't make the assumption that they will learn this stuff from others; the odds of that happening are pretty slim. It should come from you, but if another close family member or friend is willing, allow them to instill these principles. More role models are always better. They are watching and learning from you every minute.

Critical Age

When Jim mentored me at the age of thirteen, it changed my life forever. *Thirteen is the prime of your life for learning and realizing the benefits of discipline.* Thirteen is the age where it all begins. It sets precedence for the rest of your life. Without someone taking the time to mentor me, it would have been extremely difficult to get to the level I am today. I would have wasted much of my lifetime, probably getting into trouble with the law or doing drugs, like many of my friends did back in high school. Discipline should be taught at an early age if at all possible, but don't shove it down someone's throat—you need to start out slowly and gradually take on more.

> "There comes that mysterious meeting in your life when someone acknowledges who we are and what we can be by igniting the circuits of our highest potential."
> *Mahatma Gandhi*

My mentor started out slowly by teaching me what discipline was all about and what it could do for my life. At first he may have taken it easy on me, but he didn't baby me—he made it clear that certain things wouldn't be tolerated, like if I was late to one of our appointments. In the beginning of our mental and physical training sessions he made it very clear to me that if I was late just one time, our training sessions were over. There would be no second chances. He didn't say it in a nice way but a very direct and stern way. His mannerisms and physical condition were that of a drill sergeant. So how could I not listen?

> "The greatest good you can do for another is not just share your riches, but reveal to them their own."
> *Benjamin Disraeli*

One of the greatest gifts anyone can give back to society is mentoring children about the benefits of discipline. If children are mentored when they're young like I was, their life will be rewarding. If you can give your son, daughter, or neighbor only one gift let it be the knowledge of discipline.

> "Children have never been very good at listening to their elders, but they have never failed to imitate them."
> *James Arthur Baldwin*

Leadership and Discipline

You wouldn't think that discipline and leadership have that much to do with each other. Yet, as you grow in your ability to control yourself, others gravitate to you.

"A leader takes people where they want to go. A great leader takes people where they don't necessarily want to go, but ought to be."
Rosalyn Carter

The greatest challenge is to control oneself. Once you gain that ability, others recognize that you have that ability and by the law of attraction want to follow your lead. You have shown by example that you are worthy of being followed.

If you continuously take yourself to new levels of accomplishment, others will want to emulate the discipline that drives you to new heights. Through practicing the virtues and mastering your emotions, you become a leader. Leaders who lead themselves are destined to become leaders of others. Leaders who fail to lead themselves will quickly lose favor and be labeled forever.

"Leadership is not a magnetic personality – that can just as well be a glib tongue. It is not making friends and influencing people – that is flattery. Leadership is lifting a person's vision to higher sights, the raising of a person's performance to a higher standard, the building of a personality beyond its normal limitations."
Peter Drucker, 1909-,American Management Consultant, Author

The following competencies and their relevance are crucial to master in order to be a really effective leader.

COMPETENCY	RELEVANCE
Can inspire and hearten the spirit.	How do you motivate and garner loyalty?
Can develop and articulate a strategic vision for the organization and communicate it in terms that others understand.	How effective are you in bringing your stakeholders in line with your strategies? If they aren't on board, you can't possibly achieve success.
Can oversee the process of strategic planning.	How do you discern how well your staff is doing as they plan and add to an overall strategic plan?
Can articulate the "mission" vision and values of the organization and act as a symbolic role model.	You are the leader. You want respect and you want credibility. How do you ignite the energy, discipline and attitude of your troops to be engaged in your mission?

Operates from a solid ethical base.	Are you honest, decent and fair? Do your actions hold up to rigorous scrutiny? Do you practice virtues?
Makes meaning.	Do you have a personal worldview that you share with others?
Has passion.	Do you care? Can you articulate and ignite others with your zeal, energy and enthusiasm?
Can envision alternative organizational structures to operate the enterprise.	How well can you think ahead, like a chess player, about your next moves? Leaders in technology are doubly blessed with opportunities to make changes to their organizations. First, they have business drivers, such as new markets or changing economic conditions. Second, technological changes are an important ingredient in organizational changes.
Makes decisions and sets the tone, manner and criteria with which other people make decisions.	How do you make decisions? How would you explain your decision-making process to others? To those on your team? To your peers? How do you judge others' decisions?
Shows diplomacy, including the capacity to perceive others' explicit and implicit agendas, to speak in "politically correct" terms when necessary and to be seen as a peacemaker, rather than partisan.	How skillful are you at handling affairs without arousing hostility? Are you the one to whom others turn for guidance in seeking resolution to conflicts? Can you see both sides?
Builds networks and alliances—operates in the political realm when necessary.	How well do you form alliances, both formal and informal?
Takes a strong stance when necessary.	What is your record for defending and maintaining a position, such as with architectural and infrastructure standards?
Creates goodwill—communicates with consideration for others' emotions and agendas and creates agreement.	As a measure, how do your activities stack up compared to the PR organization in your enterprise or the PR activities of other internal groups such as HR? How well do you understand your audiences and how do you imbue a consistent stream of PR?
Shows creativity and the ability to think inside and out of the box.	Does your style encourage imaginative thinking and lead to innovation? Do you find another way to get around the hill, to paraphrase a campaign battle?

Designates time and resources toward research and development.	Technology leaders are frequently caught in a bind: they are constrained on budget and resources, yet they must blend new technologies together in imaginative ways. How do you allow for R&D and learning?
Shows logical, analytical thinking.	Can you think logically? Can you envision sequences? How do you discriminate between ends and means?
Can find problems.	How well can you view a wide array of data and frame the problems to focus on which can provide the greatest leverage for organizational success?
Can execute.	How are you judged and how do you perform in getting the job done? How about managing and leading others to get their jobs done?
Can uphold high standards of professional and personal excellence.	How well do you know the business you're serving? What standards do you recognize and how do you uphold them? Do you communicate your standards to your employees and your customers?
Can delegate to internal resources and outside experts.	What is your management style in delegating responsibility and authority? How well can you enroll resources?
Gathers data well.	How well can you gather appropriate data to conduct organizational espionage when necessary? How do you shift through volumes of quantitative or subjective forms of information?
Tends to act rather than react.	How proactive are you? Do you instill proactive thinking in your group?
Evaluates for decision making... does not have "analysis paralysis."	How do you measure decision making? Can you see the pros and cons? Are you able to see the consequences of your actions?
Can shape, mold and impact an organization's culture to create high performance.	How well do you create a culture of high performance? Do you inspire and energize the whole community?
Creates opportunities for reward, recognition and renewal.	What is your style and its substance for rewarding positive behavior and results?

Applying Leadership Competencies

Here's an exercise that will go a long ways towards developing your leadership skills. Each day, look at one competency, one element. Contemplate that element. To get started, ask yourself these questions:

❏ Who do I know who is good at this?
❏ Have I ever heard of someone who was good at this? Does any movie or book come to mind?
❏ Where do I stand in regard to this competency?
❏ How could I improve?
❏ Do I have any false ideas or assumptions that block me from achieving this competency?
❏ Where am I strong in this, where am I weak?
❏ When I really did this well, what did it feel like?

As you journey along the road of improving your leadership skills, you will find your life changing, your influence growing and your area of control increasing.

ACKNOWLEDGMENTS

To Leticia Gomez for being a great friend and believing in me. After working with large publishing firms for over twenty years, it's refreshing to work with someone in this business that is genuine and sincere.

To my brother Howie. Thank you.

To my friend Roger Bengtsson (www.super-self-discipline.com) for his support, feedback and conviction in my discipline mentoring program.

To my friends Tom May, Mark Gray and Rich Webster.

To Steve Tobak, my managing partner at Invisor Consulting LLC (www.invisor.ne) for providing me with the 10 Tips to Becoming a Great Schmoozer.

My Contact Information

If you are still having difficulties holding yourself accountable, feel free to contact me to discuss your issues:

• Mobile: 818.404.9248
• Email: harris@harriskern.com

I would prefer you call—I am a bit old-fashioned and prefer to hear your voice while you discuss your challenges with me. When it comes to dealing with sensitive issues, email is not always the proper vehicle to use.

ABOUT THE AUTHOR

Harris Kern is one of the world's leading life and organization mentors. Harris has been mentoring people (www.disciplinementor.com) and organizations (www.disciplinetheorganization.com) for over thirty years to attain the highest level of efficiency. He helps individuals develop key skills such as self-discipline, leadership and EQ (communication, relationship management and interpersonal). He pioneered the *Discipline Mentoring Program* and *Professional/ Personal Growth Program (P2GP)*. Harris is a master of self-discipline and an acclaimed author and publisher of over forty books, including:

- DISCIPLINE: Six Steps to Unleashing Your Hidden Potential
- DISCIPLINE: Training The Mind to Manage Your Life
- DISCIPLINE: Mentoring Children for Success
- DISCIPLINE: Take Control of Your Life

Harris is recognized as the foremost authority and consultant on practical guidance to solve management issues and challenges. He is a frequent speaker at business, leadership and management conferences. His client list reads like a who's who of American and international business: Standard and Poor's, GE, The Weather Channel, SONY Corporation, NEWS Corporation, Warner Brothers, Hong Kong Air Cargo Terminal (HACTL) and hundreds of other Fortune 500 and Global 2000 companies.

Mr. Kern is the founder and driving force behind the Harris Kern Enterprise Computing Institute (www.harriskern.com) and the best-selling series of IT books published by Prentice Hall. The series includes titles such as:

- IT Services
- CIO Wisdom
- Managing IT as an Investment

As founder of the Enterprise Computing Institute, he has brought together the industry's leading minds to publish "how-to" textbooks on the critical issues the IT industry faces.

APPENDIX A: LIFE MATURITY MODEL

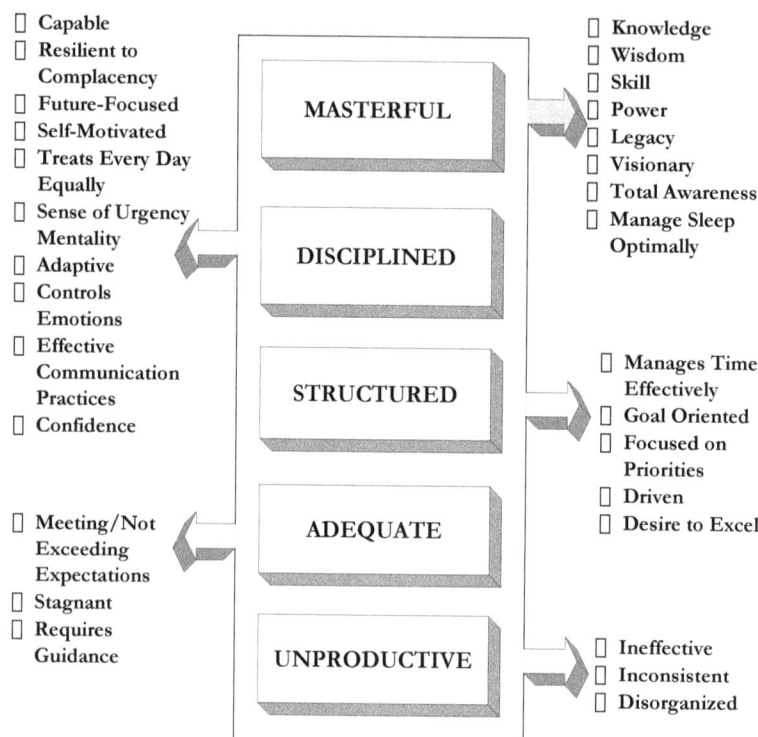

MASTERING YOUR LIFE

◻ Capable
◻ Resilient to Complacency
◻ Future-Focused
◻ Self-Motivated
◻ Treats Every Day Equally
◻ Sense of Urgency Mentality
◻ Adaptive
◻ Controls Emotions
◻ Effective Communication Practices
◻ Confidence

◻ Knowledge
◻ Wisdom
◻ Skill
◻ Power
◻ Legacy
◻ Visionary
◻ Total Awareness
◻ Manage Sleep Optimally

MASTERFUL

DISCIPLINED

STRUCTURED

◻ Manages Time Effectively
◻ Goal Oriented
◻ Focused on Priorities
◻ Driven
◻ Desire to Excel

◻ Meeting/Not Exceeding Expectations
◻ Stagnant
◻ Requires Guidance

ADEQUATE

UNPRODUCTIVE

◻ Ineffective
◻ Inconsistent
◻ Disorganized

LIFE DEVELOPMENT

APPENDIX B: TIPS TO MANAGE YOUR EXPENSES

Below are tips on how to effectively manage your expenses.

Car:
❏ Buy a car that's fuel-efficient and reliable.
❏ Buy the car you want over the Internet—you can save several hundred dollars.
❏ Don't rest your foot on the brake pedal or clutch while driving—not only does it put unnecessary wear and tear on your brake and clutch, but it also wastes gas.
❏ Don't carry unwanted weight in your car—the heavier your car is, the more gas you waste.
❏ Maintain your car on a regular basis—have your oil changed every 3,000 miles.
❏ Rotate your tires regularly—if at all possible, rotate them every time you change your oil. Many places won't charge extra for that service.
❏ Change your car's air filter frequently. A dirty air filter can waste a lot of gas.
❏ Make sure your car tires are inflated properly. It saves a considerable amount of gas.
❏ Observe speed limits. It saves gas and prevents you from getting speeding tickets, which are quite costly.
❏ Avoid unnecessary stopping and braking.
❏ Accelerate slowly and smoothly—this saves a lot of gas.
❏ Wash and clean the inside of your car at home. You won't throw away your hard-earned money at a car wash. Besides, it's a good form of exercise.
❏ Take public transportation as often as possible.

Social:
❏ When socializing with friends, don't show off by frequently picking up the tab.
❏ Don't go to evening movies—attend morning/afternoon matinees—you'll save half on your tickets.

Cooking:
❏ If you cook a casserole or lasagna, make enough for several

days. This saves time and money on your utility bills.

❑ Make sandwiches and snacks and bring them along when taking a long car ride or when you're waiting at the airport for your flight. Airport food is quite costly.

❑ Plan and cook your meals based on the deals you get from the grocery stores (look religiously through the weekly sales flyer).

❑ Cook more meals at home.

❑ Bring your lunch to work frequently. Avoid going out to lunch regularly.

❑ Make your own coffees—stay away from gourmet coffee shops.

Home:

❑ Don't have the heater running 24-7 in the winter (wear more layers of clothing).

❑ Don't leave the water running when you're taking a shower. Wet yourself quickly, then turn the water off. Soap up your entire body then turn the water back on and rinse off.

❑ Make sure you fill up the washing machine each time you wash clothes. Don't run the washer and dryer for only a few items.

❑ Don't constantly open the refrigerator door or leave it open for a prolonged period of time.

❑ Don't leave the water on while washing dishes. Rinse them first, then turn the water off. Soap them down and then turn the water back on and rinse them off.

❑ Cancel the cable or satellite stations you do not watch.

❑ Turn off the television when not watching.

❑ Buy energy-efficient appliances.

❑ Shut vents in unused rooms.

❑ Always turn off the lights when you're not using a room.

❑ Eliminate unused magazine subscriptions.

❑ If possible, relocate to an area with a cheaper cost of living.

❑ Use Skype for long-distance calls.

❑ Review your cell phone charges—remove services that aren't being used.

❑ Don't own a pet. You will save money on food and veterinary expenses.

❏ When using the dryer, cut dryer sheets in half. They will last twice as long.

❏ Replace all your incandescent light bulbs with fluorescent lighting.

❏ If you have a cell phone, don't pay for extra features (e.g., text messaging).

❏ If you have a cell phone, disconnect your land line. There is no reason to pay for both—unless it's a separate business line.

Insurance:

❏ Pay your car insurance semi-annually or annually. Insurance companies charge more if you pay monthly or quarterly.

❏ Do some research before filing an insurance claim. Don't submit a claim unless it's at least twice the amount of your deductible. If your deductible is $500.00, do not submit a claim unless it's substantially more than $1000.00. Typically, insurance companies will raise their rates after one incident—but you may want to check with your agent to find out what the impact on your overall bill will be.

Credit:

❏ Don't leave your credit card numbers active with online accounts—it's easy to forget about them and a subscription you may not necessarily want to renew will have already renewed itself automatically year after year.

❏ Apply for credit cards that offer 0% interest charges.

❏ Get a credit card that offers you reward points—but does not charge you an annual fee.

❏ If you're in severe credit card debt, call your credit card company and ask for a rate reduction.

❏ Improve your credit score. You can save hundreds or thousands of dollars on interest when purchasing a home or car.

❏ Pay off the balance of your credit card each month. Do NOT incur new debt. You should use your credit for all purchases if you get airline points or cash back.

Computing:
❏ Don't leave your computer on when not in use.
❏ Turn off the power on your printer when not in use.

Banking:

❏ Never do business with a bank that charges bank fees (e.g. checking account fees). Find a more customer-friendly bank that offers free checking and no maintenance or finance charges.
❏ Avoid ATM fees. Only withdraw cash from machines approved by your bank.

Shopping:

❏ Don't spend big money spoiling your children. There are many activities you can do inexpensively—besides, they would rather have your time than your lavish gifts.
❏ Avoid impulse buying. Plan ahead every time you spend.
❏ Limit gift-giving.
❏ Make a list when you go shopping and always stick to it.
❏ Many name-brand shampoos are expensive—add water to your shampoo to get more uses.
❏ If you haven't done so before try shopping online with amazon.com. It could add up to substantial savings.
❏ Shop at discount stores like DSW, Target, Ross and T.J. Maxx.
❏ Buy generic medicines.
❏ Don't go to malls or shopping centers for entertainment.
❏ Buy bread at a bread outlet store—buy a few extra loaves and freeze them to save on gas.
❏ When purchasing a major item, use cash as a negotiating tool. All vendors' eyes light up when they see cash.
❏ Don't buy snacks or water at the airport; purchase them from the grocery store beforehand.
❏ Don't buy snacks at convenience stores; purchase them at grocery stores.
❏ Buy items in bulk when they're on sale—especially products that don't spoil.
❏ Buy generic brand products at your favorite grocery store or from other well-known and popular stores (e.g., Wal-Mart,

Target).
- ❏ Stay away from the malls—shop at outlet stores.
- ❏ Do not purchase magazines or newspapers. Read them online or go to the library.
- ❏ Don't buy extended warranties, especially on appliances: most of the time they never get used.
- ❏ Book your flights in advance.
- ❏ Use ebates, a free online coupon website. You can get cash back when making purchases.
- ❏ When purchasing items offering rebates, make sure you keep your receipt and submit the rebate form.

Health:
- ❏ Don't smoke, drink alcohol or do drugs.
- ❏ Don't drink soda.
- ❏ Cancel unused health club memberships.
- ❏ Cut back or eliminate altogether fast foods or microwaveable convenience meals.
- ❏ If you take daily medication, instead of getting a monthly refill, ask your doctor for at least a three-month supply.
- ❏ Consistently exercise and manage your eating: you will remain healthier and save on medical expenses.
- ❏ Brush your teeth at least twice a day and floss daily. You will save on major dental expenses.

Miscellaneous:
- ❏ If you sign up for a new service which has signup fees, ask them to waive it. Eighty percent of the time, they will.
- ❏ If you live close by to a library, go there. Utilize their free services (e.g., Internet, DVDs, movies, magazines, social opportunities)
- ❏ Manage your vacations. You don't need to take extravagant trips each time you want to get away with the family.
- ❏ Don't spend money to de-stress; find alternative methods. Going on an expensive vacation each time you feel too much pressure is not the answer. The debt you incur will outweigh the 1-2 weeks of temporary relief.
- ❏ Get DVDs from Redbox for $1.50 per rental. NEVER buy a DVD.

APPENDIX C: INDIVIDUAL QUESTIONNAIRE

Personal Information

Tel #: _____

Email: _____

Height: _____

Weight: _____

Birth Date: _____

Age: _____

Relationship Status: _____

      Kids:_____

           How old: _____

           Living with you: _____

Address (own/rent): _____

_____

Work Status

Job Title: _____

      Employer: _____

           How Long: _____

Self-employed: _____

      Industry: _____

           How Long: _____

Initial Goals

- _____

- _____

- _____

Challenges

-
-
-

I. Dreams/Vision

When do you establish your goals?
❏ New Year's Eve, your birthday or some other occasion?

_____

_____

How do you manage your goals?
❏ Do you memorize your goals or write them down?
❏ Do you establish detailed milestones with due dates?
❏ Do you plan thoroughly?
❏ Do you hold yourself accountable?

_____

_____

How successful are you in accomplishing your goals?

_____

_____

Do you "hope" a lot or do you make things happen?

_____

_____

Are you constantly learning in order to reach your full potential?

_____

_____

Do you concentrate on one task or do you multitask?

_____

_____

List your most critical priorities. Do you currently abide by those priorities?

_____

_____

Do you indiscriminately say yes to everything/everyone?
❏ Do you keep your commitments?

_____

_____

How would you define success (personal & professional)?

_____

_____

Do you enjoy your work?
❏ Is it challenging?

_____

_____

What are your career objectives?
❏ Where do you see your career in 1 year/3 years/5 years?

_____

_____

What activities and/or hobbies do you enjoy?
❏ How much time is spent on these activities or others?

_____

_____

Do you have any phobias?
❏ Are their things that can hinder you from accomplishing your goals?

_____

_____

Do you dwell on the past?

_____

_____

Are you a risk-taker or risk-averse?

_____

_____

II. Drive/Attitude

On a scale of 1-10, where 10 is the ultimate level of discipline, where would you categorize yourself?

_____

_____

How do you respond to setbacks, obstacles or down days?
❏ Do you look for something positive when you're in a negative situation?

_____

_____

Do you manage time effectively?
❏ Do you procrastinate?
❏ Do you watch too much TV?
❏ Do you spend too much time in traffic?

_____

_____

Do you consistently motivate yourself?
❏ If so, how?
❏ What motivates you?

_____

_____

What are your primary strengths?

_____

_____

Are you energetic?

_____

_____

Are you comfortable in your surroundings?

_____

_____

What are some of your bad habits?
❏ What efforts have been applied to eliminate the bad habits?
❏ How much time is being wasted on these bad habits?

_____

_____

Describe your personality. Are you outgoing, quiet, antisocial, or sociable?

_____

_____

Are you patient?

_____

_____

Do you have a "Type A" (driven & energetic) or a "Type B" (laid back) personality?

_____

_____

Are you stressed out all the time? What stresses you out?

_____

_____

Are you creative?

_____

_____

III. Structure/Routine

What time do you go to bed/get up?
❏ What gets you out of bed in the morning?

_____

_____

Are you punctual for appointments?

_____

_____

Are you structured or unstructured?

_____

_____

Describe your daily routine in detail (24-7). Account for every minute. Document your current routine Monday-Sunday for any given week. Also note the time that you think is wasted. Please customize/complete the table below.
❏ What time do you get up (during the weekday and on the weekend)?
❏ What time do you go to bed?
❏ What time do you eat breakfast?
❏ What time do you shower, prepare clothes?
❏ What time do you leave for work?

❏ What time do you arrive at work?
❏ Do you go out for lunch, and if so, for how long?

_____

_____

IV. Communicating/Relating

How well do you manage business relationships?

_____

_____

How well do you manage personal relationships?
❏ Are you people-oriented?

_____

_____

Do you spend too much time with family, friends?
❏ Are you preoccupied with any family issues?

_____

_____

Do you feel that you're an effective communicator (written, verbal, email)?

_____

_____

Are you a nervous individual? What makes you nervous?

_____

_____

Are you a worrier?

_____

_____

Are you insecure?

_____

_____

V. Health

Are you in good health?
❏ Do you have any health limitations?

_____

_____

Are you athletic?

_____

_____

Do you exercise?

_____

_____

Are you a healthy eater?
❏ Do you manage your eating habits effectively?
❏ Do you diet?
❏ What do you eat throughout the day?
❏ How often do you eat?

_____

_____

VI. Finances

Do you save money?
For emergencies?
For a major purchase?

_____

_____

Do you live from paycheck to paycheck?

_____

_____

Do you manage your money effectively?
❏ Budget planning?
❏ Investments?
❏ Monitoring expenses?

_____

_____

Are you in debt?
❏ Credit cards?
❏ Cars?
❏ Student loans?
❏ Mortgage?
❏ Other?

_____

_____

VII. Miscellaneous

If you were an animal, what would that one animal be? And why?

_____

_____

APPENDIX D: LEADERSHIP QUESTIONNAIRE

How do you motivate and garner loyalty?

_____

_____

_____

How effective are you in bringing your stakeholders in line with your strategies?

_____

_____

_____

How do you gauge the effectiveness of your staff?

_____

_____

_____

You are the leader. You want respect and you want credibility. How do you engage the energy, discipline, and attitude of your troops in your mission?

_____

_____

_____

Are you honest, decent, and fair? Do your actions hold up to rigorous scrutiny?

_____

_____

_____

Do you have a personal worldview that you share with others?

_____

_____

_____

Do you care? Can you articulate and ignite others with your zeal, energy and enthusiasm?

_____

_____

_____

How well can you think ahead, like a chess player, about your next moves?

_____

_____

_____

How do you make decisions? How would you explain your decision-making process to others? To those on your team? To your peers? How do you judge others' decisions?

_____

_____

_____

How skillful are you at handling affairs without arousing hostility? Are you the one to whom others turn for guidance in seeking resolution to conflicts?

_____

_____

_____

How well do you form alliances, both formal and informal?

_____

_____

_____

What is your record for defending and maintaining a position?

_____

_____

_____

Does your style encourage imaginative thinking and lead to innovation? Do you find another way to get around the hill, to paraphrase a campaign battle?

_____

_____

_____

How well can you view a wide array of data and frame the problems to focus on which can provide the greatest leverage for organizational success?

_____

_____

_____

How are you judged and how do you perform in getting the job done? How about with managing and leading others to get their jobs done?

_____

_____

_____

How do you know the business you're serving? What standards do you recognize and do you uphold them?

_____

_____

_____

What is your management style in delegating responsibility and authority?

_____

_____

_____

How proactive are you? How do you instill proactive thinking in your group?

_____

_____

_____

How well can you create a culture of high performance? How do you inspire and energize?

_____

_____

_____

What is your style and its substance for rewarding positive behavior and results?

_____

_____

_____

How well do you scale in terms of juggling multiple balls and wearing multiple hats?

_____

_____

_____

Can you identify specialists, consultants and third-party "trusted advisors" who you may need to call for assistance, advice or to hire for their consulting services?

_____

_____

_____

What's your track record in attracting top talent, keeping them motivated and developing staff?

_____

_____

_____

How well do you set expectations and how fair are you perceived as being?

_____

_____

_____

How do you infuse vitality in an organization and identify the next generation of leaders?

_____

_____

_____

Do you know your company's "Big Rocks" when it comes to customers? This is similar to knowing what business you're in, but the question goes further. You want to understand how your business is held accountable by its customers.

_____

_____

_____

Who are your partners? Who should they be? How well do you develop mutually-beneficial partnerships?

_____

_____

_____

Can you relate to different groups and different individuals?

_____

_____

_____

Can you relate to different personality types? Are you a team player? Are you trustworthy?

_____

_____

_____

Do you build win-win solutions? Can you bring conflict to the surface in order to resolve it?

_____

_____

_____

How do you use humor, or how could you be more effective with humor, such as with storytelling?

_____

_____

_____

Are you viewed as centered? Are your emotions in balance, or are they driving your thoughts and actions? Can you be a leader whose emotions are out of control and create a long-lasting, healthy organizational dynamic?

_____

_____

_____

How do you motivate people?

_____

_____

_____

What are your outside activities and how do they relate to your position?

_____

_____

_____

Are you fair and consistent with others? Are your values communicated and understood?

_____

_____

_____

How ethical are you? How do you judge compliance with ethical questions?

_____

_____

_____

Do you deliver on commitments? Do you operate with decency and respect for others? Do you care about others?

_____

_____

_____

Do you have the stamina, self-esteem and wellbeing to do the job?

_____

_____

_____

What is your willingness to share information, power, credit, resources and wisdom?

_____

_____

_____

How do you channel ambition to constructive modes? How do you demonstrate passion and instigate zeal and enthusiasm in others for the work at hand?

_____

_____

_____

Can you make meaning through stories and use of metaphor that translates complex ideas into terms people understand?

_____

_____

_____

How do you characterize your courage to take the right actions?

_____

_____

_____

In the fast-paced world of technology, how do you judge, value and measure patience, especially with constant demands for project completion?

_____

_____

_____

Have you done a SWOT (Strengths, Weaknesses, Opportunities and Threats) analysis on yourself? How do you match opportunities to maximize your talents? How do you seek feedback on your performance? How do you give feedback?

_____

_____

_____

How do you stay abreast of new material? How do you grow? How do you encourage others to grow?

_____

_____

_____

What are your interests outside of work? How do you draw upon them to enrich yourself? Your organization? What will you say on your deathbed?

_____

_____

_____

Upon examination, how do you exert self-discipline? How do you recognize an even emotional keel in others? How do you sharpen the saw?

_____

_____

_____